JEAN TINDLE

WISDOM

of the

GRAND
MOTHERS

Tips for Living From the Realms of Love

DEDICATION:

For Hazel and Rose and all of the wise women

CONTENTS

INTRODUCTION

The inspiration to write about my grandmothers came from my women's circle. All of the circles I have been involved with are about connecting once again with the Divine Feminine, and creating a sacred space for healing and transformation. They are a place to go for support without judgment. They are a place where as women, we can find our voice, be witnessed, and allow balance back into our lives. They are a place to find solace when tragedy strikes, and to celebrate the joys of each woman's life.

In this particular circle, we were doing some work with the feminine lineage of our families, a thread that has run through our many years together. The original idea was to work more with the Cosmic Grandmother aspect of the feminine. What transpired for all of us as we began to focus on this work, however, was the more personal relationships we had (or did not have) with our own grandmothers.

As facilitator of the circle, my good friend and mentor Susan Lipshutz, went with the flow of this and suggested that we sit for five minutes per day over a month's time with photos of our grandmothers. She advised us to just ask a question or simply listen for any guidance they might wish to impart to us through these meditations.

Susan gave us a quote from Sobonfu Somé, an African medicine woman, to ponder as we worked with these energies. I am paraphrasing here — this is my memory of the quote. "Your ancestors prayed you down for a reason. They are not who you think they are, and the reasons may not be what you think."

Almost as soon as I began the process, using the only pictures I could find of each of my grandmothers — Hazel and Rose — their clear voices began to speak to me both individually, as the women I knew in my life, and often as One — the voice of the Cosmic Grandmother. It was as if they had been waiting for me to connect with them. I opened my heart and their words flowed freely through my pen. I found my five-minute meditations turning into an hour or more as I wrote down all of the information and stories I was hearing from these "grandmother voices."

As I continued posing questions each day during my meditations, and as the time I spent with my grandmothers grew, I realized that the wisdom I was receiving and the energy of this tremendous "Grandmother love" coming through Hazel and Roses' words, might be of benefit to a larger audience.

This book is a result of my conversations with my grandmothers over a period of three months. Through my work with them, I have come to some deep understandings about my own work in this lifetime as well as a deeper understanding of the women who were my grandmothers in life. In a larger sense, I have begun to understand how much we, as women, are and have been restricted by the culture and time period in which we live. I am speaking here of Western culture because that is my experience. I cannot presume to speak to or for those whose cultures are vastly different from my own.

I have asked the Grandmothers to clarify Somé's fascinating quote "prayed you down." Here is what they answered in the voice of One Grandmother.

The lineage of love is never broken. We as humans will pray in a personal way for love to come to us in the form of a child or grandchild. In the larger sense, we are offering our prayers for a lineage of souls (who are all connected to us) to be able to have the human experience — to learn, grow, expand and love in this third dimensional life on Earth. We are not who you think we are. We are much larger than the bodies or names you knew us as. We are connected to you throughout ages of linear time and we are and were connected to you as both your physical grandmothers and that aspect of love that is pure, whole, non-judging, and defined by you as Feminine Love.

The word "pray" has become much maligned in your world as various groups have claimed and defined it as theirs. It too, is much larger and more expansive from where we sit. It is a calling out from the heart to the Universe for connection to that Source Light that we all are. So to "pray you down" is to connect to Source and allow another aspect of ourselves, in the form of a child, to come into our experience.

During this time, another image our women's circle worked with was a piece of gold silken thread that was to represent the thread that ties each of us to certain lineages throughout time. Expanding on their words about prayer, my grandmothers spoke of this golden thread.

To expand on this connection through prayer, we must go into another image that may be unclear to you. At the beginning of this circle project, you were given the image of a golden thread to meditate with in relation to the lineage of Grandmother love. This image of the golden thread is tied to the long line of physical connections to your own grandmothers. It stretches throughout time (as you know it) or dimensions (as we now understand it to be) in an unbroken line of love and human experience. It is the thread that connects us through all of the stories and lives that make up our experience as souls. The many souls who are having "separate" experiences are all aspects of Divine Love. They are having all experiences in all dimensions, within all infinity. This is a large and expansive thought, so the golden thread is a simple image of light and love stretching back through one's lineage as we experience it on this plane.

From my first tentative connections with these remarkable beings, who I like to think of as my Grandmothers in angel form, to the moment when I felt an ending had been reached, I sat, pen in hand, taking notes on all I was hearing, and not quite believing what I was experiencing. Yet I know deep within my heart that this connection was real, true, and from the highest aspect of Love.

Throughout this book, I begin each chapter with a "question of the day" that I posed to my grandmothers. I received answers in several different ways. First, I received answers from Hazel and Rose, speaking more or less as the individuals I knew as my grandmothers in their physical lives. I have noted these speakers as Hazel or Rose. The other way they answered was as one voice, speaking from that great Cosmic Grandmother that is a Divine Feminine aspect of Source. These answers I have designated with a (G) or Grandmother. This was done for clarity but also because I wanted to honor the wisdom of my own feminine lineage and allow my grandmothers the voices they didn't have in their lives. When there is no designation, I (Jean) am speaking. (I have also put my words in italics to add clarity for the reader.)

BEGINNING THE JOURNEY

12/3

Today I am beginning my meditations with my grandmothers. I am not sure what to expect, but I have their pictures in front of me. I have set up a small altar to honor them during this time, and I sit facing the altar, not sure of what to ask. Even at this early stage, I feel anticipation. I feel in my heart that this is the beginning of a huge piece of soul work. I ask, "What is it you wish to say to me?"

(G): We will speak through you to the many. This is your gift, the translation of all things into language that sings. It is our cherished wish that you see this and know this.

We are both speaking because we are one. There is no distinction any longer. We are the golden thread from which all is woven. You are a part of this thread, as is all of creation.

Why have you "prayed me down?"

(G): To love you. There is only now, and it is filled with only love. Look at the thread in your mind, follow it Home and back. It is unbroken. You are eternal and we are a part of that. Hazel and Rose. Tree and Flower. Cancer and Scorpio. Water. We are the voice of the Divine Feminine, and we can speak to you now through the channel of the Grandmothers, Hazel and Rose. We are love.

We will speak to you each day and help you to weave a story. It will be a journey. It is everyone's story — you are everyone and everyone is you. We will become clearer as you listen. The golden thread has no beginning and no end. Remember also that the Divine Feminine and Masculine come together as one in the eternal now.

I ask again, why have you "prayed me down?"

(G): The Grandmothers have spoken. It is time to stop being small and fading into the background. You have brought unique gifts to the planet — use them. Your words, your heart, your connection to Creator, your knowledge of other dimensions and realities — these are your gifts.

THE QUESTION OF LINEAGE

12/4

I gaze at the photo of my maternal grandmother Rose, surrounded by her two daughters, and I am reminded of the three fates. They smile out of the picture at me from some fictitious time. I wonder about lineage and choices. I have chosen these women as my family and they love me, and have loved me as best they can. I have chosen not to physically carry forward the lineage, and I wonder if this makes some sort of rift in the woven pattern of matrilineal lines.

I have had many more choices in my life than my grandmother did, or even my mother. Have I made the ones that served me best? I can hear Grandma Rose whisper to me from beyond any place I can understand.

Rose: You have chosen freedom. In the end, whatever choice you make serves your soul. There are understandings you carry that are beyond the small ego mind. From these understandings, you are guided in all of your choices, whether you know it or not.

The matrilineal line is never broken. It extends from the feminine aspect of Divine wholeness and is carried in an unbroken line of Love. That is the truth of the golden thread. Anyone who has been touched by your love is a part of this thread.

Now, I sit and contemplate Grandma Hazel's picture with tears streaming down my face. I had not anticipated the power of this simple practice — connecting to your lineage of blood. I have spent so many years releasing those aspects of my family that were painful and disruptive, and I have forgotten the tremendous bond of love that connects me with these people.

Grandma Hazel is silent today. She is at peace. There is nothing to add or subtract. She has taken her place with the angels. So far from the "backbone of the Methodist Church" that she was in her life. I want to know more, but today she is silent and at rest.

THE THREAD OF THE JOURNEY

12/5

I am still trying to define this project of meditation with the Grandmothers. So I ask today, "What is the thread of this journey — reconciliation, reunion, remembering, coming back to where you began with a different understanding?"

(G): We will speak to you as one today. The journey is circular in nature, or spiral, as you have come to understand it. We were there at your beginning and we watched you grow. We saw you turn away from yourself and from this place of truth and wisdom, and we watched you come back again. It has been necessary for you to turn away from your human roots to seek the more exotic lineages that call to you. In the end, you must come back to a place of understanding of why you took this human form at this time and in this body. You must understand why you chose what you chose and what you can do moving forward.

What you have accomplished is no small thing. You woke up in the middle of a comfortable life and realized your spirit's call. We have come at this time to assist you in moving forward. We were not able to move this way in our lifetimes — with the freedom you have. Understand that we are not who you think we were.

Think about the gardens we planted, and know us from those memories. We made (and make) things grow. We watered them many times with our tears, yet from those tears came beauty and sustenance.

From this vantage point, we can incorporate the Goddess into our awareness although it is not what you think. We are one between us, and we are also one with the masculine side of ourselves.

What is the journey I can go on with you?

Trinidad has joined me today and she is also my grandmother. Trinidad Vilches Pezo is the grandmother of a shaman I studied with in Peru. She taught him everything he knows about sacred plant medicines in the jungles of Peru. Her medicine included guidance from the pink dolphins of the Amazon. At the age of approximately 104, she jumped into the Amazon to join the dolphins, and this is where her spirit resides. I did not have the honor of meeting her when she was alive; however, she has come to me many times during shamanic journeys and given me experiences and advice that have been pivotal to my growth as a human being.

Trinidad is reminding me of the journey we took into the river — the freedom of swimming effortlessly through the water, following the flow of the river, dolphins at our side.

(T): You have many grandmothers, stretching back to the beginnings of your incarnations on this body of Gaia. In some ways, you are your own grandmother, passing down through the eons you have been here in this place. The journey is the river.

Why are we speaking of the matrilineal?

(T): It is time to balance the mother and father. Go back to the fire and the water. Go back to the Earth and Sky. Go back to the original grandmother. She is earth and water. He is fire and sky. Masculine and feminine — one cannot live without the other in this beauty. There is another kind of beauty beyond, but you are here to enjoy this Earthly beauty. It is simple and it flows on the construct of time until there is no time, only eternity.

Why do we keep jumping around?

(T) Because you are thinking from an ego place. In the continuum, you are many and you are one. We are telling you all of the truths of many eons and the infinite. It is all being said at one time which is now.

GRANDMA ROSE

12/6

Today, Grandma Rose has asked me to tell her story.

Grandma Rose loved to learn. She was born with a keen and hungry mind. She was the last of five children and the only girl. She was born a Mennonite, and her parents were farmers. As a girl she loved to read and she did well in school. She wanted to go to college and become a teacher. Her father refused to send her because she was a girl, and there was only enough money for the boys to go.

So she watched as, one by one, her brothers went to college and graduated. She swallowed her anger and put herself through secretarial school. As a woman, in the 1920s, she did not have many options for advancement at work. Marriage was the only way to advance both socially and economically. Again, she swallowed her anger, got married, and had two daughters. Through her daughters she was able to fulfill her dream of college. Both of them went, graduated, and continued their education throughout their lives.

Grandma Rose lost her keen and hungry mind several years before she died. As her memory failed her and her inhibitions fell away, she began to let out all of the anger and frustration she had subdued all of her years. She would scream at many of the people she had loved throughout her life. She spewed venom at most of her caretakers. She hung on tenaciously to life — long after most of her functions were gone. She had an iron will and nowhere to go with it. Trapped in her body at the end, her anger seemed to fuel her until her death.

In her garden, Grandma Rose grew stunning roses of all kinds and food for her family. She was a good seamstress and baker (her pies were something to dream about). She did her best with what she was given, but deep down she was disappointed and angry.

I can feel her now through the words she speaks to me, and her essence shines forth in all she says. She is now in a place of understanding and her strength has softened into acceptance and love.

I ask, "Is there anything more that needs to be said today?"

(G): We see your worry and feel your longing for our presence. We are here to guide you. We are here to let you know that we have always seen you. Bright star. Loving heart. Passion for so many things. Blazing your own trail. Though your path has been twisted, you have come to a place of peace, even though you can't see it yet. There is no need to fear. The continuum is infinite and there is no goal to achieve. We will assist you in reaching your heart's desire. Just know that there has been no wrong choice. Be at peace. We are your loving grandmothers, Hazel and Rose.

CHAOS

12/6

There has been a flood in my basement and I am finding myself in chaos, not able to get anything done. I have resisted moving in with my partner Robert, who lives two hundred miles away. I know it is the next step in my life and yet I resist. Still, I continue to sit with the Grandmothers.

(G): Out of this chaos will come unimaginable beauty. You will create something that touches your own heart and in that way, touches others. You have a good man right now; allow him into your heart fully. Do not put limitations or preconceived ideas into your now. Do not resist the love that comes your way or shut yourself inside. Your space has become too small — literally and figuratively — to inhabit your life fully. Life is wide and deep. Age is not the limitation you imagine. You have spent a lifetime gathering wisdom. Look both within and outside of yourself and see the love flowing back to you. We love you beyond all imagining. We dreamed the unique soul that you are to come into a body, to experience and emanate the love we feel when we see your light. Expand into the large, infinite space that we know you can. There is no right or wrong choice. We say this again so you will remember.

Your space is too small. Look at it like a plant that needs to be re-potted so the roots can expand.

Are you talking about moving?

Hazel: Your world is small right now. Move into the larger world. Consider where love lives. It is everywhere. Expand into whatever new space you find, geography is irrelevant. Simply make your world larger. Expand. Stretch. Grow out of your perceptions.

WATER/RESISTANCE

12/7

I can feel your presence here right now. It makes me smile. Since I did not come with a specific question today, I am not hearing your words. What is it you wish to tell me today?

(G): We wish to talk of the Mother, of her waters and what you are doing and experiencing at this time. You have not understood the water. It has always scared you because you cannot control the water. Even as a child, you were resistant to the pull and flow of water. You were calmed at a distance but afraid to dive in. You stood on the shore because it was safe and because it was a place of peace. The crystals of the sand spoke to you. The waves beckoned and you kept your distance. One foot, maybe two, would tentatively touch the water.

Now is the time to dive deeply into the Ocean of Being without resistance, without fear, and without any sight of land or safety to come back to.

You must trust that you can swim, float, and dance in the waves. You will not drown. Drowning is resistance, not flow. The water has come to you in many uncomfortable ways because, although you honor it, you do not embrace it. You stand at a distance and watch. We are inviting you to immerse yourself. Get wet. Let the waves take you away from the shore for a while. Remember the songs of water how they play.

For the last twenty years or more I have done ceremonies to honor and heal the waters of the Earth. I grew up by Lake Michigan and the water has always provided me with solace and calm. It is where I go when there is nowhere else to find peace. I have always felt that ceremony is the least I can do to show my gratitude. Alone or in community, with drums and fire, with tobacco and flowers, I honor the waters and say prayers for the healing of the lakes, rivers and oceans. I ask about the ceremony I do with water.

(G): The ceremony you perform is good, and it honors what you know of water. We are inviting you to go deeper, to allow yourself the freedom of abandonment in its truest sense. Complete abandon, nothing left, nothing to do, nowhere to be but in the dark depths of the ocean. As Trinidad has said, you can breathe underwater. It is only a matter of remembering. In the water you are free. Take a breath.

Begin to communicate with the creatures of the sea. Spend time with your shells. Listen for the tones the water makes when you let go of resistance.

We are here today to teach you about water. It runs in your veins, and it makes up your cells. It is an energy that speaks in your body. All of the stuck places, or places of pain, are simply resistance to life, to your own body, and to the waters.

Embrace your life. Do not stand on the shore and watch. The water is warm, come on in. There is only love.

HAZEL SPEAKS ABOUT ABANDONMENT

12/8

Hazel wants to speak today. She wants to tell me about abandonment and how it can make you feel small and unworthy. I ask her to tell me her story.

Hazel: When I was a girl in Cordova, Alabama, we lived in this small town in a big white house. My father was a dreamer who was always looking for adventure and big ideas. He did his best for my brother and me and my mother. He would tell us stories of the faraway places he wanted to see and the exciting adventures he would have there. He was a great storyteller, and my brother and I would listen to him in the evenings as he spun another life, filled with exotic places and people. We both wanted to see those places, and traveled in the stories with my father as willing sidekicks to his adventure.

One day I sat on the porch waiting for my father to come home. I was ten years old, and my brother was eight. We waited side by side until it got dark. My mother was late getting dinner that night. When she called us in, there were tears in her eyes. She told us that our father was not coming home.

I am wondering now why I did not ask Hazel more about her life while she was around. Sobonfu Somé is right. Our ancestors are not who we think they are, even in life, and so much more so in Spirit. There is no one left alive to tell me these stories, so I must listen to them from Spirit.

Hazel: My mother dried her tears that night, squared her shoulders, and never spoke another word about my father. He had simply vanished from our world. When we would ask about him, we would get the back of her hand.

He became one of his tales — a fascinating adventurer who had passed through our lives for a short time and left nothing but stories behind.

For the longest time I would sit on the porch waiting for him. I couldn't quite believe he was gone. It hit my brother even harder, and in some ways, he left with my father. As soon as he became old enough, he left us just as my father had done, and we never heard from him again.

I am talking to you about loss and abandonment because you are carrying this burden down through the lineage. You have chosen to be the last of this physical line, as a way of ending this thread [of abandonment]. It is something that has played out through my life, through your father's life, and now through yours.

I never forgave myself for my father's abandonment. My mother did the best she could for my brother and me. She turned our home into a boarding house, and she took in laundry and cooked for the neighbors. We were that poor family without a father. I carried that shame. When I met Frank and he offered to take me up north for better prospects, I went. My mother came with me because I could not bear to abandon her too. She lived with my new family for the rest of her life.

My final abandonment, and the most painful one of all, was when my son John died in WWII. The pain of that loss stayed with me for the rest of my life.

I am telling you this story to help you see how you take the losses in your life and how you blame yourself. To help you see how you let abandonment, or more importantly the fear of abandonment, keep you from allowing yourself to fully love someone. You fear that everyone you love will leave you, and your life has borne this out to some extent. You cannot see that love has no limits in time and space. It moves throughout the infinite and is with you always. You know this in your head but not in your heart.

It is time to let this fear go, to heal the long line of pain, unworthiness, and sorrow. There is nowhere love can go that is away from you.

For many years I felt that if I had just been a better person, my father, my brother, and even my son might have stayed around.

I even married a man I was not in love with because if he left me, it would not tear me apart. We were together for fifty years. When he died, I was sad, but I did not feel abandoned. I was able to move forward. Your father and John were, and are, my soul mates. They were the ones I loved beyond measure in human form.

From the spirit world, I can see the patterns and weavings we, as a family, have created. I see your thread, golden and pulsing with life, ready to move forward once again and stalled with fear. There is nothing to lose. Those people you loved who have moved away from you in physical space are still loving you. There is no end to love. It is alive in your heart and will be forever.

In this Now, at this place in your human life, move forward with the understanding that you can complete this legacy of abandonment, of pain, of fear, and of loss. It is a choice, and I have told you this story to deepen your understanding of what you carry. Lay it down, my love, and move more fully into life.

What is your advice to me right now?

Hazel: Do not live in your losses. We have just begun this process [this book]. Dwell in the love and not the loss. You have created this series of abandonments to come to the place of understanding. Be at peace with this process. It is not a test, and it can help you move forward. That is what we are here for. We are with you and always have been. We say this over and over because it is essential for you to know that love does not die. It just changes form. Look at the golden thread and work with it. It expands into All That Is.

THE GOLDEN THREAD

12/9

Talk to me more about the golden thread.

(G): It is your connection to all who have gone before you in this human existence. It is not one thread but many. The lives you have lived are woven and intertwined. Your soul is much larger than you imagine and contains many aspects — lives within lives, ancestors of many lineages. Life is wide and deep and encompasses a vast territory. All that you are and will be lies within you in this moment. The golden thread is a part of the grid that your soul travels.

It is helpful to understand one thread at a time when you are in the limited space of the body. Within you, though, are all of the threads belonging to your soul grid. They can be accessed by going within. Any meditation practice will connect you first to your personal [i.e., this lifetime] thread for exploration and healing, then to the wider grid of your soul, and finally to the realization that all of the golden threads of light are one light. It is a process, or a soul's journey, to come to this realization and finally to merge into it. We are pure consciousness that has stepped down in vibration to assist you. Just as we prayed you down when we were in human form, so you have prayed us down as spirits.

Using the image of the thread is just a tool to further understanding. Grandmothers are weavers. They hold the strands of light together through their strength and their love. As we tried to guide you in life from our more limited perspective, so we are guiding you from beyond life.

We are asking you to understand where you have come from so that you may move onward. We are asking you to transcend where you are and have been by going back to your beginnings in this body, as this hologram called Jean.

What is it that I need to do in this Now?

(G): You have begun the process of going within. Follow this process. For many years you have been connecting and reconnecting with your spirit. This information is a continuation of that process without some of the distractions you have created for yourself these past few years. We understand distractions because we experienced this pattern in life. It is time, however, to move forward with more trust in your own spiritual mastery. No more distractions.

Know, though, that your body and spirit need fun and play. There is a difference between fun and play and the kind of distraction that serves as an aspect of resistance to life. Do not feel shame or guilt for anything you do. There are choices to be made. You will be given chances to grow into the transcendent light of your Being. It is your choice to go or not to go, to take the chances or not. Either way, there is only Love at the end.

From this place, we have no regrets. In life, we were both limited by our choices. We did not follow our hearts' desires. We did what we could in the times we chose to live in. We prayed you down to continue and fulfill some of our own desires — to be what we could not be. In life we wanted more for you than we had ever imagined for ourselves. From this place of spirit, we can see and understand the patterns of many lifetimes.

I don't even know what questions to ask you. How do I form all of this wisdom and knowledge into a story to assist others?

(G): Do not worry about the form. Simply ask the questions and we will answer from love. It will all flow as long as you stay out of resistance and simply write. At this point in the process, just remain open and in your heart. Feel the love that we have for you sent down through the single thread of this lineage. Almost everyone has grandmothers who love them. It is universal. The connection will come from there. We will speak to the Feminine throughout our time together, and how it is so much more than your limited understanding of it.

Start with the simple questions that are common to all of humanity. From there you will build a foundation. We will help you create a perspective from a fuller, more multidimensional place. You do not need to mention this; it is simply an understanding at the base of all of this. Questions such as: "Will I find love?" "How do I find love in my life?" "Will I be happy?" "How will I find a meaningful way to sustain myself?" "What is my purpose for being here?" "Will my children be okay?" or "What can I do for my children?" can be asked of us.

You may think it strange that we have included children here. You do not have any physical children in this lifetime, but a broader perspective is necessary for the survival of your species at this time. It is the responsibility of all to care for and create a joyful existence for the children of your human dimension. Directly or indirectly, the children must begin to dwell in a love-filled space. Children understand this but may not be experiencing it. The question of how to love the children is an essential one. It will go a long way to balance existence on Earth in the third/fifth dimensional shifting that is happening now. You are surprised that we speak of dimensions. We are not who you think we are.

Begin with the questions we have given you. Add some of your own. We are beyond proud of who you have become and we await your presence each day with joy and love.

Remember the Christmas Eve service where you first felt the presence of God/Goddess? You were singing "Joy to the World" in the church choir and you actually felt the joy. This is how we feel when we speak to you each day. We are sending you love beyond love from the place of eternity.

THE PERFECTIONISM TRAP

12/11

I skipped my meditation yesterday and I found that I miss this time. It is a time spent wrapped in love. It is a good way to start the day. I am asking today for both the questions and the answers.

What do the Grandmothers wish to say to me today?

(G): We can feel the low-level fear that accompanies you in this month of stillness. You see the small picture of a business that has not, so far, been abundant. We see the potential that lies within your heart — so much to give to the world, so much left unspoken. We are inviting you to speak up. Now. You have chances that we never had to reach out to people across the world. Our human world was small. Yours is vast. It goes beyond the human and into galactic dimensions.

We are assisting you to be more human and to bring your message through on a level that will touch the many, not the few. You have understandings that go beyond what many humans can hear. This is neither good nor bad. It is simply a place where you are at this moment.

Get in touch with the human in you. What do you struggle with daily? The nagging fear we spoke of earlier is one example of your struggle. It keeps you small and limited. We see you as you are. There are no limits.

Do not be afraid. We can feel your fear today.

Rose is speaking. "I spoke earlier of perfectionism being a trap. It is something I struggled with all of my life. I needed to please my father. I needed to be better than I was. I never felt like I was good enough. My brothers were the focus of the family. I was loved, but largely I was just decoration.

To make up for this, or to get noticed, I felt I needed to be perfect. My house was perfect. When I baked I followed the recipe perfectly, never adding a grain more of salt than was called for. When I was in school I got good grades, had perfect attendance, and perfect handwriting. I was a good girl and never caused any trouble. As a result, I was angry my whole life.

There was nothing out of place in my life. I felt like I was suffocating all of the time. I wanted to get out and travel, make a name for myself. Dance. I could have danced. Mennonites don't dance.

I spoke to you of perfectionism being a trap. It is the worst kind of trap because you wait for the perfect moment to do anything, and your life is over before that perfect moment comes. You wind up feeling inadequate because nothing is ever perfect in your messy human reality. Stop. Being. Perfect. It is a goal that cannot be achieved and it will keep you stuck — paralyzed with the fear of making one misstep. You will never measure up to some self-imposed ideal of perfection.

Get out and live your life. It will be and is messy. Write your book and say whatever you want. Some will resonate with your words and some won't. This is not important.

Take yourself out of the prison of perfect. I am speaking to you from a place of true perfection — from the beyond, where all is love. You will understand this soon enough. In your human form, allow yourself to be messy and unafraid.

There is no recipe. Just add what makes you happy, stir, and put it out there.

MANIFESTATION AND SPIRITUALITY

12/12

I seem to intuitively know when something deep or intense is about to be imparted. This happens today as I sit in meditation. My mind is moving all over the place like a bouncing ball, trying to resist the words of the Grandmothers. I am thinking about abundance and spirituality, but no question is forming.

(G): Why are you resisting us today? Do not think that you have figured out what we want to say. We are not who you think we are — just as you were told in the beginning of this process. We are feeling your question on manifestation and spirituality, and we will attempt to answer.

All religion and spirituality comes together in the end; all of the words used to describe these terms, all of the rituals performed, they all fall away, and what is left is the light of love.

This is not new. We are speaking to you in one voice because it will bring you to a better understanding of this place of love. You have been here, [this place of pure Love] touching the Source energy,

and there are glimpses of this within your human framework —
times when you feel the edges disappearing. When this happens,
you begin to merge with this love essence. In this place it becomes
easy to love, easy to be kind, and easy to cooperate with others.

The practice of manifestation has become just another way to
accumulate "things." This is not the intent of this practice or of
this law. The true intent is to open the flow of Universal Love and
allow it to spark out from each human being. Practicing the "law
of cooperation" might be a better way to focus your attention.
"How can I reach out?" "How can I create an atmosphere of love
surrounding me and flowing outward?" and "How can I help?"
These are questions that we would suggest you ask. Once the flow
is open, the natural abundance that is inherent in these questions
will make itself known to you in miraculous ways.

Don't resist this. There are many "yes, buts" connected to this
knowledge or the resistance to this knowledge. When we prayed
you down into this existence, we were not calling you into a life
of struggle and limitation. We were calling you because all things
beautiful come out of the love we have for you. When you open
to receive this love without any filters or shields, abundance is a
natural byproduct. All you need is provided; your heart's desires
are provided.

*Hazel and Rose, what were your struggles that you haven't
mentioned yet?*

(G): We would like you to rephrase the question. There were no
struggles, just experiences that our souls had not yet had. In the

illusory nature of human existence, things have been separated into good and bad. In the wider perspective from which we speak, these experiences were just part of the great human existence. Dreams we dreamed to fill us up. Dreams we dreamed to coincide with the other souls with whom we interacted.

Duality can be a trap, but right at the moment in your human form, it is a necessary one. Awareness is what you can strive for if you like and the charmed moments when the edges disappear and you experience a small part of the Oneness that is Source/ God.

Why do I not have questions today?

(G) You are experiencing a state of grace — a state of peace in which you can simply rest. There is no worry or fear in you today. Enjoy this and know that you are cared for.

Can I ask about Mary (Divine Mother)? (In working closely with the Feminine aspect of the Divine, I have found that the one image that resonates for most of those with whom I work is Mary. Most people can relate to Her as Mother. She is, for me, the Divine Mother and her energy informs much of my healing and teaching work.)

(G): We will speak to you about Mother. She is the great mother of us all. She has many aspects and many names. We are in Her and She is in us, whether we are in human or spirit form. People are only just beginning to understand the Divine Feminine aspect of God once again. Nurture and sustenance, foundation and support, union and cooperation: these are the feminine traits that must be balanced for the next phase of humanity's growth.

ABUNDANCE AND LACK

12/13

What do the Grandmothers have to tell me today?

(G) Your fear is back today. Again, it is a low-level background noise. It keeps you in stasis. You are missing the abundant nature of life. Seeing money leak away, seeing friendships wane or go dormant — this is your fear manifesting itself in front of you. The words "money is energy" or even "love is energy" can pass through your mind in understanding, but your heart has yet to feel this truth. So you keep yourself in fear, and what you see in front of you is what you fear.

You are trying to figure this out. It cannot be done with the brain. The brain is set up to solve problems, so that is what it creates for itself.

Rose: Where I felt most abundant and free in my life was in my garden. It was full of good things to eat and flowers for beauty. I could get my hands dirty and enjoy what I had planted on a daily basis. In my garden I forgot my disappointments. I couldn't worry about all the things I didn't have when I was surrounded by so many good things to eat and so much fragrance.

In my garden I was present and whole. I was powerful when I took tiny seedlings and nurtured them to full ripeness. Sometimes I would just stand in the dirt in the middle of the garden and take in the peace and sense of accomplishment I felt. Here I was queen. Here I was capable. Roses responded to my touch. String beans grew crisp and plentiful. I was happy in my garden.

Think about abundance as a garden. Think of your life as a garden. In it you are queen. All around you are the seeds you have planted. Get your hands into it and get dirty. You must care for the seeds to make them grow lush. You must pull out the weeds of doubt and fear. In this moment, look for the beauty that is there. Find the little patch of green and focus on that. Focus on the energy of growth. Nurture that. When a weed of doubt appears, yank it out with gusto. Find the people and activities that feed the green growth. Those friends you have loved — keep loving them and be grateful for the time you spent together. Stay connected. They are the strong root system that will feed you, have fed you and have helped you to grow. Be grateful for them. Relax into this lush green garden you have created. It is just winter now. The plants are asleep.

Hazel: I wish to speak to you about what you perceive as spiritual beings "selling out." This is the most destructive feeling you have had since we began this process. When you see someone, even someone you may feel is "not that spiritual," speaking up and becoming successful, be happy for them. They are doing the best they can, and they are putting themselves out there for the world. The people they touch are people who will be blessed by their touch. They will become abundant, or not, based on their own beliefs about this. It is not up to you to judge them.

I speak from love and from the knowledge that this judgment is toxic to your own soul. Think of the term "no limits." It is not a concept easily grasped by someone limited by a human body. However, it is the truth of this Universe in this dimension that there is really no scarcity of anything. There is always plenty. You limit yourself by harboring these feelings of judgment about spiritual people making money, or putting themselves out there for the world to see. Be happy for these beings; let them touch who they touch. Cooperate with them. Reach out to them if they are in resonance with you. If not, just be happy for them.

There is no limit to the abundance to be found when you get in touch with what excites you and offer it up to the world.

There will be people who judge you as you have judged others. This is not important. You can understand and have compassion for those people because you have had these feelings yourself. Let them be and stay in the excitement of your own passion.

The energy of money flows in this way — not by grasping on tightly to what you believe is yours, or believing that money (abundance) is limited in some way. The energy of money flows by creating a cooperative and supportive sense that all people deserve money (as the energy of abundance), and by being happy to help people when you can. Everybody wins. Until everybody wins, nobody wins. Do what you can to feed your own excitement, and everything else flows.

Think of my table on a Sunday. Overflowing with food made with love by my hands. There was always plenty. This is an image to take with you of abundance and love. It is everything. You chose us as a family to give you this touchstone. Remember it whenever you feel that "not enough" feeling.

(Trinidad): I am sending you a vision of the jungle right now. It is just another reminder of the lush abundance that you have experienced in your life. It is within you, in the plant spirits you have taken in. It is always with you. When you have clean water, lush plant life, and a creative spark, you have all you will ever need. If you want a picture of "green energy," conjure up your memories of the jungle and the rainforest's song.

MOVEMENT

12/15

What do the grandmothers have to tell me today? Who wishes to speak?

(G): We will speak to you today as one. We are speaking of movement, and for you that will mean moving your home. You have become stagnant where you are and you grasp at small things when there is a wider world to explore. This world is both inner and outer to you and will open when you make the commitment to move. You are not tied to any physical place on this Earth. Many places will touch you and anywhere is home when you have realized the Home within. The Earth is your home and wherever you walk is sacred.

As you open up to explore the many options for home, you will find that it is not necessary to stay in one place all of the time. As you open to moving and movement of all kinds, doorways will appear for you. As you flow, so will things flow to you.

Do not cling to Chicago. It has served you well. You have grown up here, and you have left much of yourself here. Your time here is coming to an end. This saddens you and we can feel your sadness and your resistance to change. Stop for a moment and remember that your true purpose here, in this holographic realm of Earth, is to enjoy the ride. It is to experience all aspects of being human.

Success does not come from anything outside of you. It is not connected to how you sustain yourself with money. It is not your job, your path, any of the things you have defined it as in the current consciousness. You do not need to be "rich and famous." Let that go. You are a star, and we mean that literally. In the Universal consciousness, you shine brightly. All of the rest is just your ego wanting to be recognized.

If playing bigger will make you jump for joy, by all means play as big as you like. If money and releasing all of your previous goals (and we mean all of them) feels more joyful, do that.

You have come to a crossroads and there are angels in all directions. It does not matter which way you choose to go. We will tell you that many doors will open for you simply by making the choice. It does not matter what choice is made.

Stop worrying about money! That is the last thing you need to concern yourself with. The open doors will allow that energy — abundant and green — to come in. You made the choice before you came in that this would not be a life of struggle. Your choice of family was made with this in mind. Your struggle has been internal and will always be — until you decide there is no longer a need for that.

In this time of reconnection with us, you have chosen to feed your soul. In a way, you are performing a soul retrieval on yourself, and we are here to provide assistance and knowledge where we can. It is our gift to you. We have always seen the very best in you. We have loved you beyond all time. We prayed you down so you could experience the mad genius of this human experience.

Do you have specific guidance for me right now?

Hazel: What are you afraid of? Almost everyone you have become close to has moved. We spoke earlier of abandonment. You cannot be abandoned when you understand the nature of Love. When you fill yourself up with love from the inside out, there is nothing that can touch you. Those who have moved on are just following their own star. It has nothing to do with you except that you called the experience into being in order to understand and grow from it.

In my human form, I felt the same pain as you. I do understand it. When you are the one to move on, you will provide the experience for someone else.

Why do I keep losing touch with those I care about so much? How can I change this pattern?

Hazel: Life is a moving, changing flow of experiences. Again, you must begin within and connect with the deepest and widest feeling of love for yourself that you can possibly feel. That changes everything. Your connections will transform. Part of the reason you lose touch is because you have completed the reason for the connection. Part of it is your own fear and abandonment issue. You may become angry with the person for leaving — even if you cannot admit it to yourself. Part of it is simply that life goes on, and in the present moment, love has presented itself in another form. Reach out to those who have been dear to you if you want to stay connected. They may be feeling the same fear you are. Someone has to reach out. Reach out in love and you will not be disappointed, no matter what the response is. That love within you for yourself becomes a beacon for all who are in resonance.

Rose: Remember to laugh. Remember your sense of humor. It will get you into a different place without moving at all. It will make movement easier.

LOVE/FINDING LOVE

12/16

I am so grateful for the love, the support and the brilliant words from all of my grandmothers and, yes, from the One. Tell me about love today. What do I say to those people who think they will never find love?

(G): We have spoken of the obvious solution — go inside and begin to find things that you love about yourself. Write down one thing each day, even if it is the smallest thing you can find. "I like the way I can raise one eyebrow," or, "I like the color of my nail polish." *(Grandma Hazel, your favorite nail color was Windsor Rose. I remember.)* Write down one thing each day for thirty days. It can be a different thing each day or an elaboration on the thing you chose the previous day. Write it down because your hands and your heart are connected, and the energy of what is written down will be subconsciously taken in by your heart. This simple practice is a miraculous way to begin.

As you continue, begin to put the pieces and sentences you have written into a whole picture. You will have an integrated whole, that you really love, beginning to form. Open your heart to the person you have written down on the paper. You are seeing yourself.

If there is resistance to this practice, there may be a deeper underlying cause for the self-doubt or self-loathing. In this case, deeper work must be done to find the cause and heal the wounds that keep you from self-love.

So many of the phrases we, as adults, toss off as inconsequential are taken into the body and energy of a child as truth. Be careful with your words. Speak lovingly as much as you can when there are children around. Here is where the seeds are planted to love or not love oneself. Even as an adult, if we are conditioned to lack self-love, we take a casual hurtful remark or rebuke to heart. We are too willing to see the "negative" comments as truth and may not even notice the positive ones.

When we truly love ourselves, comments or actions that may be perceived as negative or hurtful cannot touch us. We understand that the person making comments or taking actions like this is in pain, and we can choose to try to comfort them or to move away. Resolving another person's pain is not the responsibility of anyone else. Acting in kindness, however, will be a natural response in one who is in love with herself.

As you develop your self-love muscle, you will radiate an energy that attracts the same love to you. You will find yourself surrounded with loving individuals and from that will naturally come the love you desire.

Many people may not be willing to put in the time and effort to begin to love themselves. There is no "quick fix" love attractor. This [loving yourself] is the way to find true and lasting love —

from friends, from partners, from your children, and from total strangers at times.

It is simple to see on paper and not so simple to undertake. It is the most important job you can have in your life. It is the true path. As you love yourself, you cannot help but spill that love out into the Universe. It is a larger field than you can imagine, and there is no end to it.

We would tell you to do this for yourself. Test it out and make it your own practice before you offer it up to those around you. If you have people asking you the question, [How do I bring more love into my life?] they are reflecting something within your own field. That is how it works.

Until you become a Bodhisattva (a being who stands at the edge of enlightenment but volunteers to return to the wheel of reincarnation to teach and assist others in attaining enlightenment), you will receive the questions and requests that are most in resonance with what is inside of you.

What is the next thing a person can do to help them find love?

When you are just bursting with the love of yourself, begin to put yourself out there more. Say hello to someone. Introduce yourself at a gathering. Ask questions of another person. Ask them about their life, their struggles, or their finest moments. Do not worry about what someone else is thinking or how you might look to them. This worry, and this manner of thinking, reflects self-doubt or a feeling of unworthiness. When you truly hold the love of yourself fully in your heart, these thoughts will no longer arise. Again, this is the work of many lifetimes — don't be hard on yourself. True self-love, when reflected outward, is characterized by genuine interest in another.

Put yourself in one situation per day, or even one situation per week, where you are in a new space, connecting with someone you don't know, or who you want to know better. Do this for a month or two and you will find yourself surrounded by love.

Remember this as well — you are surrounded by love in this moment. We are loving you, and all of those who have gone before us are loving you madly. The angels of heaven are loving you. God/Goddess is loving you. You are surrounded and uplifted with love. We can see your heart expand as we say these words.

Close your eyes and imagine the golden thread that connects you — heart to heart — with those who have gone before. This golden thread separates into many strands and weaves a web of love out into the far reaches of the Universe and beyond. There is no beginning and no end to this love. We are here to represent a small piece of this thread — a piece that you can grasp within your human form. Almost everyone can feel and understand a grandmother's love. Those who cannot see or feel it in their current lives may be beyond your help or the confines of this book. Many others will be able to grasp the concept of Grandmother Love. It is a big concept, if we do say so ourselves.

Can you each give me some words of wisdom that define love?

Hazel: Remember the time I took care of you in Chicago when you were so sick? You were in your twenties and trying to be so cool, and I rubbed Vicks on your chest and made you chicken soup. That is love.

Rose: I taught you how to sew. It took all of the patience I could muster and then some. You were never all that good, but I praised every effort you made because I knew you would find your own way to shine. That is love.

THE HEART

12/19

I ask the grandmothers to speak to me today about my own heart in the hopes that it will translate to the heart of the many. I have just had a massage and asked my massage therapist and energy healer, Moira, to work on my heart chakra. Afterward, she told me about the depth of what she saw and felt — she saw a deep vortex and felt my inner child lurking behind my left scapula. She could not get the muscle on that side to move, no matter what she tried. She felt that whatever I put in place there (the tightness behind my heart) was put there for protection. She even tried to come at it from under my left arm but could not get the arm to release completely so that she could move it. I, of course, was trying to control the process.

I had a sense during the massage of how I have closed myself off from love out of the fear of being hurt or abandoned. The depth of the issue, as my massage therapist explained it, was surprising. She never did get underneath the left scapula (the right one moved instantly).

So, my question to my grandmothers today is, "What is it that I am protecting myself from? Why can't I open my heart?"

At first I don't get a sense of them. I am trying to listen for what I want to hear. Then:

(G) We are inviting you to dive in deeply and explore why you must control your life so tightly. When you realize that you have created all of the heartbreak you have experienced, you can begin to change things. Feel the way your heart feels right in this moment. There is resistance in you, which is why you are having trouble hearing us speak. We are right here around you and with you. Creation and control are two different things. One involves flow and the other involves resistance. This distinction is important to understand if you want to proceed with your life in a more coherent and joyful way.

It is another case of learning from the inside out that love begins with you, with your heart, and with your own reflection in the mirror. This is one of your major life lessons, and it is resonant with many, many people on this Earth at this time.

To proceed, you must proceed in love. It will not work in any other way. It is a planetary goal as well as a personal goal. You have an awareness of your own personal work, or you would not have asked Moira to work on your heart center. You have repeatedly gone back to this place, your heart, to learn about love in human form. You have created many experiences of the lack of love, and you have created a few where love was very present, and very pure.

You have chosen us to speak through you because when we were with you physically, we both represented love to you. There was never any doubt in your mind that you were loved. This was your choice. You created such an insular and comfortable place of love within your family that you found it hard to go outside that place.

The family was there to provide you with love, but you did not develop a sense of loving yourself and the necessity of that.

Your experiences since you left the confines of the family (and as they died and "left you" one by one) have been of seeking someone to fill that hole, to fill you with love. Your responsibility for loving yourself was forgotten temporarily.

Do not go into blame over this. You have realized a very core reason for why you are here — to remember true love. The closer you get to it, the more you resist. You do not have to have your heart broken anymore. Cherish those who cross your path and, when the time comes to let them go, let them go in the knowledge that love never dies. It only changes form.

What is this depth of pain Moira saw? And when or how did this protective shield (this is how I see it) on my heart come to be? How can I remove it?

My brother, Rob, has come up for me in this moment. Did I always know I would lose him? We were very close as children and through our teenage years. During his first year of college he developed the first symptoms of the schizophrenia that would plague him the rest of his life. In 1996, at the age of forty-two, he committed suicide. His death left me devastated but also brought me to the spiritual path I walk today. Whatever our agreement as souls has been, I am grateful to him as both my teacher and my friend.

Hazel: Your brother had a very complex mission set out for himself. He had many choices to make and each choice set up a different chain of events. Originally you were to come in together as twins, but he hesitated a moment. [Rob and I were born thirteen months apart.] You had that potentiality [twins] laid out and in fact, in one particular dimensional reality, you were and are twins.

His lifetime here was to experience and learn about choices and their consequences. You were more certain about why you were here. You both had a plan to do great work here together. You have known about this truth from previous ceremonial and meditation work you have done. He chose not to go through with this work, and that broke your heart. This was the origin of the shield on your heart in this lifetime. (And what my massage therapist had seen as the physical block or shield around my heart)

Note: The heart shield my grandmothers and I are speaking of here is an energetic "picture" that has appeared in me and others with whom I have worked. It appears as a crescent moon shape over the left side of the chest. It feels like a metal plate and can be removed in layers over a period of time. Sometimes, as in my case, it takes years and possibly lifetimes. We (the two women shaman/priestesses I have worked with over the years) have created a healing technique that works well with this. We apply spikenard oil to the "shield" and use stibnite to loosen the shield. Tibetan quartz and rose oil to both clear the space and replace light into the cleared area.

Hazel: The pattern or template of the heart shield has been in place for many lifetimes before this. You have already done much of the work to release the shield; the physical body, however, is resistant to change. When this pattern is broken and you can fully open your heart, your work of this lifetime will be finished. I will specify here that this is your personal work. You can choose to do much more for the planet.

One indication that your heart shield has begun to crumble will be when you let your loving partner Robert fully into your life — when you both find a compromise and allow yourselves to be happy.

(G) We will go back to your brother.

Those early choices he made to separate himself from you set off a chain of despair and self-loathing that followed him until his death. Part of the schizophrenia was caused by him being torn in two by his decision. None of this was conscious.

Know that he has great love for you at this point in time, and you two have spent many lives together. As soul mates, and in many different roles, you have traveled through space together for a long time. He cannot speak through this pen — he has other work to do and other places to rest.

At this point a quote from Andrew Harvey comes to mind, "If you're really listening, if you're really awake to the poignant beauty of the world, your heart breaks regularly. In fact, your heart is made to break; its purpose is to burst open again and again so that it can hold ever more wonders."

How does this understanding help others?

(G): There is no one alive who has not placed this shield, or one similar to it, over their heart at one time or another. Many times it will resolve itself over time. When the heart breaks over and over, it will harden into a shield and appear as you have seen it. You have already given the answer above. We will tell you to use the quote about the heart breaking in order to open more fully.

When viewed in this way, you can keep the space soft and avoid taking in the hurts you receive in the physical and emotional bodies. Call on the love that always surrounds you from Source, and you can navigate the "heart wounds" more easily. Awareness, breath, and assisting one another will eventually make the open heart less vulnerable to these wounds. The simplest answer, and the most difficult to act on, is to love one another as we have loved you. There is only love.

THE DIVINE FEMININE
AND GATHERINGS

12/20

Today I ask about the upcoming Solstice and a way to honor the energy of the Dark Goddess (by this I do not mean evil, I mean the dark, rich Earth Mother, and the silence and darkness of the winter season in which we can rest).

(G): We are with you as you begin to experience inklings of how the Divine Feminine will come to be in this new era of Oneness. You have heard whisperings through other people of the longing for women's gatherings. In our era, we gathered around church or around a common goal such as cooking, sewing, weaving, and the things that were "appropriate" for women to excel in. This is seen as negative in your current dualistic view of reality. These gatherings were, however, a time where we could find peace and joy in each other's company. We, as women, shared a commonality that was comforting and supportive, even as it kept many of us limited and restless.

In the evolving choices that are available to you in this Now, there is a longing to go back to some of those collective and supportive ways. You have partially filtered out the repressive nature of any human being, being forced into a specific role because of gender. We would suggest that a new way could be created — for women to form cooperative group efforts in many realms of possibility. Those who choose the very crucial task (joy) of raising the children can do so in a cooperative way with the burdens and the enjoyment alike being shared among many. Those who choose to engage in business can do so in cooperation with their sisters so that all may thrive. And those who choose to "have it all" will have their choices eased by the fact that many others share the burden within a cooperative effort among all women.

The aspect of the Divine Feminine that will be most essential going forward is the art of cooperation. The lush abundance that is before you in the guise of Mother Earth will be at the base of your ceremonies at the Solstice and at other sacred times during the year. Honor this Dark Goddess — Mother Earth in winter — by going into the silence and connecting to each other through breath, rest and loving presence.

WORKING WITH CHANGING ENERGETICS

12/22

I have missed another day, and I can really feel the missing of it. I am hungry now for the wisdom of my grandmothers while they are willing to visit me.

I have called you in, and I felt you yesterday during the Solstice. You were very present as I performed a ceremony with the women in my circle. The energy of the Solstice was not galactic yesterday as it was last year. It felt very Earth-centered and grounding. I know that the Galactic energy lies within as well as outside of us. Perhaps this next year (2014) will be more about the Universe within and how it evolves on the Earthly plane. I'm not sure I even know what the questions are anymore. I am asking today for your wisdom in whatever way you wish to give it.

(G): We would like to speak more about loss today. We can feel the collective sadness of a year of losses in your world — old ways of being, old ways of feeling safe, many people who were finished with life and chose to leave this existence. Many on your Earth plane experienced loss last year, and this may have seemed surprising to you. In the climactic end of 2012 where the fifth dimensional Earth began to interact and integrate with the collective "reality," many people expected something cataclysmic, or at least very obvious, to occur. In fact, a huge event did occur, but it was very subtle and witnessed by relatively few as an obvious shift. You experienced this, as did many of the people who were ready to evolve. For a large portion of your planet, life went on as usual — or so it seemed.

In 2012 the resonant field on Earth amplified, and it will continue to change as the years progress. Since then, nothing has felt the same. For example, you can now perform an action that you have done a thousand times during your life, and the outcome, or emotion associated with the outcome, can be vastly different. The way this manifests for those who are not necessarily aware of the shift in energy is a feeling of anxiety or unease, sometimes even anger, because although everything looks the same, it feels very different.

Energy is amplified and will continue to amplify, and this can feel very uncomfortable to a physical body that is unaware. Physically, this energy can even short-circuit the nervous (electrical) system in the body. The heart is particularly susceptible because it is the center that must be completely open and in movement (active compassion) during the next phase of this "new age."

We are aware of the pejorative nature of the phrase "new age" in some places on your Earth. It is, however, definitely a New Age, and the sooner that is embraced by the many, the easier it will be to birth it into actuality. As the fifth dimension continues to integrate with this collective reality, it will become more and more apparent to those energetically sensitive individuals when they occasionally drop back into a lower vibrating reality. The world will appear completely different depending on where you choose to put your attention. This has always been the case, there is just more awareness around it now.

How do we move forward in this awareness?

(G): The meditation you did the other night for the waters, and specifically for the area around Japan [Fukishima], is a good example of how to move forward. There was an awareness of the problem and its magnitude, and there was no fear around it for the duration of the meditation. There was no attachment to a particular solution (since there currently is no solution that your brain can comprehend). There was simply the creation of a field of possibility for a new solution to come in. A sense of love and support was sent to those dealing with the problem directly and also to the nature spirits who have been depleted by this tragedy. Most importantly, this meditation was done as a group effort. You had only a small group, and yet a powerful field was created. We cannot stress this enough.

It is the group, the collective, the resonant community coming together that will create an Earth of pristine beauty once again.

Anything and everything is possible when people join together as a loving, cohesive whole. You cannot currently perceive what happens in the quantum field when you send out these thoughts and prayers. You have only seen an inkling of the possibility and promise of this. We promise you that you will continue to be amazed as you walk this new field of consciousness together. We are right beside you, cheering you on.

Hazel: I want to give you a word of encouragement about speaking up and not giving up. Doors are opening for you in ways that you do not yet know. Your words can potentially touch many, and it is essential to your soul that you put them out there at this time. It does not matter what medium you choose — just do it with as much courage and determination as you can muster. I watch you hesitate and I feel your fear. This is not necessary, and it can be overcome at this time. This is an agreement you have made time and time again — to teach, to write and to spread the word of new things. You are a priestess/priest — inhabit this role and you will do great things. It does not matter how big or small the arena — just do it to feed your soul and fulfill your spirit. I am loving you from this place and cheering you on when things are tough. We, your grandmothers, are giving you words, but they are your words too. They would not exist if you were not the channel through which they can come.

I am not hearing Rose today except as the One voice. I can feel the energy of her namesake plant, and I can almost smell the fragrance of roses. In this midwinter silence, the smell of roses is enough.

THE FLOW OF CREATION

12/27

It has been five days since I last wrote with my Grandmothers.

I could feel you during the holidays, and the sweet memories of love and family surrounded me at all times. I have no specific questions today. Tell me what you would like me to speak of in this coming year. How you would like me to arrange these words in order to speak clearly to all I will touch? And, tell me about this need to be alone when I am with people I love.

(G): The need to be creative is one of the deepest desires of human beings. You have defined creativity narrowly in the past. It is much deeper and wider than you imagine. Periods of solitude are necessary for anyone to hear the whisper of their own hearts. Connecting with energies outside of you, with the Great Source of love, requires times of meditation and solitude. Some beings are more eager to have this connection than others. It is neither good nor bad, it is simply the way you are wired when you come in. Many people desire connection with others all the time because they have come here to learn to be with others. Relationships are important and are a main reason we take bodies. When things go out of balance — interaction in relationship to solitude —it can feel uncomfortable. Or sometimes you come to Earth for only one of these experiences, and this is fine too.

We would say to you personally that relationships and solitude must strike a balance. Too much of either throws you into resistance. You feel this resistance as sadness or frustration — two sides of the same coin. We would ask you to examine the resistance when it comes. What is it that you are resisting and why? Or another way to look at this is to simply accept the state of being you are in — desiring either solitude or relationship — without questioning. Be in the place that you are with acceptance and grace.

You can do great things if you can just accept the flow of creation as it comes. You also need the experience of being in relationships (even when it is difficult) because this is the good soil from which you grow. It feeds the creative front more than you know. Your primary relationship at this time is with Robert (*my partner*). (*Note: My father, brother and partner are all named Robert. Yeah, I know.*) It has always been Robert in this lifetime. We will tell you that this is no accident. The name triggers in you a deep sense of why you are here.

I ask them to explain.

The connection to this name, which was broken early on by your brother, was the initialization of a large piece of work on the nature of love. It was the potential for a movement, which Robert [brother] could not sustain. His nervous system was wide open to energy in a time when this type of openness and connection was not understood or acknowledged. He needed to use substances to dull his sense of being that was electrified all of the time. He went too far with many of his choices as we have said before, and his soul must now repair the damage of complete disconnection from his purpose in this lifetime. He could not have survived the immense amount of love required to create a movement.

Look at some of the other beings you have connected with either personally or through media. Examples we can give you are Oscar Miro-Quesada, Panache Desai, Sai Baba, and the Dalai Lama. These are just examples of the level of love you and your brother had planned to bring forth on Earth. The timing was right but you had agreed to do it together and this has not occurred. This is not a failure. It is just another road taken. The fact that both of you viewed it as failure has colored both of your lives. He has dealt with it in his own way and you have dealt with it in yours.

You are now back to a place where you can bring forth some of what you had planned to do when you came here. You cannot do it alone. You have chosen your partner Robert to be your support. It will be a different kind of support but no less essential for the next phase of your life as Jean. Let this Robert into your life, and let him love you as only he can. You will be amazed at what will blossom when you allow this relationship to grow. It can be a major teaching for you in letting go of resistance — in allowing flow into your life. We are watching you and we can feel your hesitation. You will not lose any part of yourself in this relationship. You will learn to love exponentially as you bloom. You will have the solitude without the sadness.

How will this personal story speak to others?

Many people have chosen difficult relationships or have resisted relationships altogether to maintain some idea of freedom or independence. What they have lost in this is the chance to love wholeheartedly and without condition. They have walled themselves off from others out of a sense that they will lose something by being in a relationship. As a result, many lonely, struggling souls feel they must create a life alone, and they must do it without assistance even when they desperately desire it. Through stories of a return to love, or of the struggles against resistance to love, they may be touched enough to overcome their own struggles. It is not really your concern to change another's path. Just put the words on the page and let them have a life of their own.

It is the same with healing work. You have the highest good of the recipient in mind and then you consciously detach from any specific outcome. It is not for you to determine the hows and whys of what will touch others. Simply put forth the words from your heart (and our hearts) to others and let them be.

We are assisting you to write at this time because we understand the delight you feel when putting words on a page. This delight is your work right now. Feel it and let it spark outward from your being. It will touch who it touches and you have no control over that.

Can I get one sentence from each of you about the coming year?

Hazel: Don't be afraid to put your heart on the page. It has always been meant to be shared with others. You are taking a giant step forward. The company of heaven is behind you, cheering you on. There is only love.

Rose: When I told you earlier to bloom, I said it knowing the huge effort it takes to coax some flowers into full blossom. The result of this effort is a beauty beyond compare. It will shine from you like the brightest star. Bloom my love, bloom.

RESOLUTIONS

12/28

It is the end of 2013, and I have given up on long lists of resolutions for the next year. I have only these two — to stop playing small and to bloom, as the Grandmothers spoke of yesterday. This is the year I put the book out there. This is the year I fill up workshops and ask for the order. This is the year I let procrastination and its root cause — fear — go. This is the year my business breaks out of its rut. This is the year I hire an assistant to do some of the tasks that I never seem to get done. This is the year of movement and ease. I feel the Grandmothers in the background nodding as I write these words.

Hazel: I am happy for you today. Your vibration is shiny and your intentions are clear. We are here for as long as you need us, to help you step up. Know that you are stepping up for all of us — being bigger in your own life than we could be in ours. We have set the stage and you are fulfilling the promise you came in with. There is no more to do than that. Whether you choose a vast stage or a small one, you can fulfill your promise now. All has been released that needs to be released, and the way forward is clear. You have only to act from a place of joy and the world of possibility is yours. Go forward and be big. I am behind you with love.

Rose: How big do you want to be?

Mastery requires that you be true to what your heart knows. It is not blustery and forward. It is gentle and kind. Mastery does not feed the ego; it simply serves the soul.

Playing big is only defined by your own level of contentment and ease and by your own feeling of satisfaction. It cannot be measured against anyone else and found wanting (or even found to be bigger and better). You do not need to seek to be bigger than anyone outside of yourself. Play big by all means, just make sure it is by your own definition and your own sense of authenticity.

When I was in the body called Rose, I measured myself against many others and always found myself wanting. There were years of striving, which left me exhausted and unfulfilled. The only yardstick is your own heart. Remember this and be as big as you like. I am the spirit of Rose and the essence of rose. I represent the Mother in these words. You will know me by the scent of roses.

LISTENING AND PROCRASTINATION

12/30

How can I best get focused on what I really want to do with both my business and my life?

(G): You must take time in silence each day to tune into your own voice. We are speaking through you and to you. However, your own voice will tie it all together. Just sitting and listening in silence without distraction on a regular basis allows enormous clarity into your life. Also be open to the surprises that arise. Do not go into your time of silence with preconceived ideas. Don't resist the surprises because you have already made up your mind about what you want to hear. From this point on, you can open a space of awareness that will lead you in surprising directions. There is no one "thing" that will make it all clear. Clarity is a progression of steps taken while listening to your own heart.

You are both blessed and cursed with many options. You look at them all and become paralyzed by having to choose the "right" one when there really is no wrong choice. This is not new to you, and it is something to take to heart. Choose an option and have fun with it. Then choose another and play with it until you are fulfilled. Do not think that by choosing one thing, another is lost to you; it may turn up later in a different and unexpected form.

For example, you are writing this book. It is something you have longed to do for most of your life. Right in this moment you are focused on this. Other things will move to the background while you finish it. It will open the rest of your business in ways you cannot foresee. But, you cannot focus on all of your future possibilities at this time because in this moment, you are focused on writing this book. Focus comes from pure excitement and eagerness to be in one space for a time. When the eagerness and excitement leaves, move on to the next thing. This does not mean procrastination.

We want to bring up procrastination again because it robs you of valuable time, and much worse than that, it robs you of vitality. You sit benumbed in front of the television for hours, and this is heartbreaking to watch. This is fear and resistance in action, and although you are aware of it, you allow yourself the luxury of indulgence. This is the most toxic thing you do — it brings about anger at yourself (which can be directed outward), it brings about a sense of hopelessness, and it feeds into your resistance to life. We are saying this not to chastise you but to help you to see how much more fulfilling your life can be without the pain of procrastination and resistance. As you know, what you do with your time is always a choice, and you have come far in fulfilling what you set out to do in this life. Be aware of procrastination because it causes you much pain and it stunts your essence.

When we spoke of moving from one thing to another and making your choices of what to focus on, we felt you jump to a place of fear about your age. There is always an infinite amount of time in each Now, when it is approached with excitement and eagerness. In the end, you are not ever judged by what you perceive as "accomplishment" in the limited human sense. You are not judged at all. You simply return to Love and as a soul, you can see all of the wonderful experiences you had and learned from in your life, and how much you brought the love that you are into the life that you lived. You will laugh in amazement at your most wonderful and experience-filled life.

We will say one thing about the next period of time coming up. It is filled with potential, and the energy of the coming year will (can) move you forward into the flow with much ease. There is no room for resistance in this year. Take the stardust and create your own world — it can look completely different by the end of next year. Open.

How can I redefine Home to include Robert (my partner)? Where am I supposed to be?

We have told you to sit in silence and open up. This question holds its answer inherently in this process. You must leave yourself open to things that you may not have ever considered before. We cannot tell you what to do; we cannot interfere with your free will. We can tell you what we see, and we can remind you to let go of resistance. Your time in your current place of living is coming to an end. The energy of the place no longer supports the light you carry. You have felt this for some time and you have resisted it. There are many places on the Earth where you can be happy, and your true home is within your heart. Let this unfold, and when the time is right to move, you will know it. As you open more and more to eagerness and excitement, you will be more and more able to move around in the world.

You are speaking as One today. Do you have any individual advice on this or any other topic so far?

Hazel: I gave up everything familiar to me to move north with your grandfather. It was that part of me that wanted the same adventures my brother and father chased after — to get out of the familiar and see something else. It was not always easy to live in the north, but your father and uncle were born there. I found great happiness in something completely new. When Frank and I went down and lived in Mexico for a few months, another wish was fulfilled. I always wanted to see the world. Mexico was as far as I got. I am saying this because in the energy of the time that you are in right now, there is much movement. As you move along with it, you will find enjoyment in the dance. There will always be chances for movement — one will pass away and another will present itself. Within the movement of this energy is your own stillness within. Within this stillness is where you can become rooted and at home.

Rose: My Jeanie, don't put limits on where you can go. Don't give yourself a list of rules and then feel guilty when you break them. Release your anger at yourself for any past fear and imagined sins. Remain open to any possibility. Expect good things to turn up each day. In one of these invitations to open up, you will find a new home. Don't let yourself be talked into going somewhere you don't want to go, but also remember that wherever you go is

Home. This is just another way of saying that you carry Home with you.

When the time comes for you to move, there will be nothing in heaven or Earth that will stop you. Stay open and engaged in your life. Remember eagerness and excitement — they are your watchwords and touchstones for the coming time.

FEELING ETERNITY AND BALANCE

1/2/2014

A new year is so full of promise and passes so quickly away. I can feel the edges of the eternal just outside of my ability to comprehend — sometimes close and sometimes so far away. I ask the spirits of my grandmothers to help me to open up my body to the eternal. In my spirit form, I understand it. More and more, I feel this knowing of the eternal in my body. More and more, I am able to feel the edges of myself dissolve and merge into the One.

(G): We are feeling a sense of stasis within you today. You are in between believing the promise of the new year and doubting your ability to rise to this promise and stop playing small. You feel hopeful, and you are looking at the failures of the past — feeling the weight of them in your heart. What you perceive as failures, however, have merely been growth on another plane. You feel you have wasted a tremendous amount of time. This is not the case as time is never wasted, and time is actually just a perception.

You wrote down today that you desire to feel eternity. To do this, you must stop being concerned with time. It is irrelevant. In the eternal space of being, this life and this body you are experiencing right now is an infinitesimal speck. The time you have been alive in your current incarnation is a blink. Do not wrap yourself in gloom about what you have or have not accomplished. This concept of time's irrelevance seems difficult to grasp. You have done much and experienced as much as you wanted. Much of the procrastination and fear you feel is leading you to have compassion for others who may feel stuck and in fear. "Time" is never wasted. It is just experienced in one way or another.

What you may want to look at more deeply is how it feels to "waste time." If you are in an activity that drains you or makes you feel numb, this is an indication you may not be having an experience that delights your spirit. If you choose to feel differently, do those activities that delight you. It seems too simple and yet it is the core of what we can teach you from this current place of understanding.

We want to speak to you now about ceremonies and how you have and will create them. Here is a place where we can see you sparkle as you work in this field. Here is where you can really make a difference for many. Here is where you and the being called Oscar [Note: Oscar Miro-Quesada, one of my primary teachers of the Peruvian tradition in which I am initiated] intersect in the heart. You have learned the importance of making life sacred from this man. He has shown you how to create a space where magic can happen for those who are open to it. More and more, the structure of reality will be shifted by the creation of ceremonial intention. As people flounder in an older reality consensus, the power of ceremonial intention will bring them peace and move them forward. Step up to this as a calling and you will feel the sparkle that you are in spirit form.

Almost anything you can conceive (and many things you can't yet conceive) is achievable through the ceremonial process. Living life as a sacred ceremony can become a choice. You can teach it to anyone and everyone. The tradition you have been given by Oscar can be made into a workable format for any area of life.

We can say we will help you to bring in the Grandmother energy into anything you choose to do. The Crone aspect of the Divine Feminine is very powerful, and when you incorporate this aspect fully and joyfully into your being, much can be accomplished. Crone is the wild woman, she who knows her own mind and is not afraid to speak it. Crone is the woman who no longer bleeds, but connects to the Earth Mother through her service alone. She passes on her knowledge to those who come after her, she offers her love freely because she knows its value. Grandmother is the Crone embodied. She lets the Divine flow through her to be of service to the people.

When we were alive, we ran the churches and supported the growth of the children. We created and brought forth pure love through our cooking and our gardens. We allowed you to grow up in the strong field of love and passed on our own strengths to you and your sister. Creating this field of love and support has been done by countless grandmothers all over the world since the beginnings of the current civilization. Grandmothers have been the rock and the foundation of many of the ways in which the Earth Mother has and can be sustained.

Look to the Grandmothers for messages of love, balance, nurturing, and sustenance throughout history. Do not discount what we were in the past. It may seem that we had limited choices, and in some ways we did. We were, however, creative and worked with the ways we were given to change the world and to allow things to progress. The Divine Feminine has never been completely undermined. She works through the subtler ways of love and nurture. She also works through magic and mystery, she brings life onto the planet, and She ushers life back to spirit. Make no mistake, we are powerful and have always had the power.

At this time the Divine Feminine will step up to her rightful place of balance with the masculine gods. You may perceive it as slow, but remember what we told you about time. The ways of masculine/feminine balance have arced back and forth through the ages. Now is a time of balance.

Is this the new ceremonial process (balance)?

Balance. Balancing the elements of Earth and Water with Air and Fire. You came in as a feminine body with the predominance of air and fire. You have in your nature the inherent understanding of balance. You have, within your structure, built a unique way of understanding how to balance. You have also brought an understanding of stillness, so this balance might be achieved and sustained. You have worked with this your entire current life, and you have shed and released much of what keeps you away from this understanding. This is a gift and it was also a choice you made before birth. Use this understanding to help others create balance in their lives. We are opening for you a way of moving forward that is in resonance with your soul's purpose. Choose what you would like to do and we will support you with the energies of heaven.

Teach people through ceremony how to get in touch with their own fonts of wisdom. Teach them to be still and to come to the point within themselves that allows them to move with grace and ease through their lives.

We remain with you in complete love.

ROOM FOR LOVE AND A SENSE OF PLACE

1/5

The grandmothers continue today with the topic of creating a new future.

(G): As you are creating a vision for the future, be sure to leave a lot of room for love. You are opening yourself to your vision, and it is easy to get swept away in the details of creation. Leave room for love. It is in all places and comes in many forms. It can sometimes be forgotten in the rush of activity that is life.

One of the things we had the luxury of doing in our time was staying at home and nurturing our children. You have no physical children, but there are many children (and grown children) who can benefit from your love. Do not close yourself off from this. Look outward in any direction and there are ones who will benefit from love today. A simple smile filled with love can change the course of history. You do not know how that vibration can reach out. You do not yet understand the impact of the energy of a smile — the pure love that can come out of the eyes and reach into the soul of another. This is the important work. When you visualize a plan of action, take a moment to step back and leave room for love.

Clarity of vision is in direct proportion to your excitement of (or fear of) that vision.

As you add breath to fear, as you breathe through any resistance you have for stating what you want, the vision will come in more and more clearly.

Don't limit yourself to what seems possible because all things are possible right now. Forget your age, forget your current circumstances good or bad, and begin to breathe into any place of resistance. This is a key and a portal, just remembering to breathe deeply through any resistance and any fear.

Part of your vision for this year is a space to do your work more fully — a place in nature, a place where Robert is there, a place where love lives. You know the place. You have the tools to create it, and many people are waiting to be a part of your vision. Listen to the whispers of your own heart. Allow people to assist you along the way. Open.

Stop hiding in your apartment. We see you and love you; we want you to expand, fed by the clarity you receive when you breathe through resistance. None of this was in our awareness when we were alive. Yet each of us walked the spiritual path that was available to us. Each of us loved and was loved. Each of us understood the role of nurturing.

I am looking at the pictures of Hazel and Rose and trying to know them as women in addition to their spiritual essences speaking to me as one voice. I remember that Hazel always had her nails done perfectly, and she had beautiful well-fitting suits. Rose created and surrounded herself with beauty — her home was spotless, there were green plants and violets indoors, and roses and vegetables in her garden. They both cooked with love and deliciousness. They raised their children to be loving, caring adults. They experienced loss and sorrow, and yet they could laugh and have a good time.

Tell me more of who you are and how you look at vision and creating.

(G): We are you. We are the co-authors of this book because we believe in you and we have been waiting for you to be ready. Keep going.

Hazel: Don't look too far ahead when you are creating a vision. Remember that Now is the point of creation. Focus on what your body wants right now. To bring your vision into the present moment, you must know the present moment. You must become well acquainted with your feelings now. You can be grateful for all that has gone before, but don't dwell in that. As for the vision of a future you, even one that is only one year away, don't create limits. To reach into the future and pull out a picture, you must leave room for life to occur. What steps to that future are making you eager and excited right now? Do those steps and see where they take you. Each day, do the steps that excite you. When you can, get someone else to do the things that must be done but don't excite you. In this way you will create a vision and version of "right now" that pleases and amazes you.

Rose: Remember to include nature in your vision. Remember to honor the good soil and green food. Remember to care for your body as well as your spirit. Remember to honor those things that feed you. Remember that in honoring us, you honor the family and what it has stood for in your life. Even as you made different choices, know that the solid foundation that was laid for you allowed you to feel safe in those choices. There was much love around you as you were growing up. This was of your own choosing. Remember those of us who supported you with love. Forgive us our sins, and remember us with love. We are here on the other side now cheering you on. This is connected to who you are right now. Your vision for the future rests on the shoulders of the past. Be grateful for where you came from and remember.

MISSING THE CLOSENESS
OF FRIENDS

1/6

I am feeling the loneliness of my solitary pursuit this morning. The question in my heart is, "Where is the closeness I had with Kay, Piper, Holly, and Maureen?" They are dear friends of mine who have moved away to follow their own paths. When we were together, we created a haven for each other to find peace, healing, laughter and love. Why can't I find that again?

(G): There are complex reasons why you came together and complex reasons why you split apart. You must remember that you are never really separated from those you love. Your time together was an initiation for all of you into the mystery school of your own soul's growth. It was intense and concentrated because it needed to happen quickly. You made the agreements — as you know — and when the initiation was over, you were (and are) all needed elsewhere. Piper had to come back briefly for the transition time that occurred in 2012. You were needed together for those moments. The knowledge and actions that occurred during that time were far-reaching and beyond your ability to understand at this time and in this body. It is information you will both use in your own ways for many years to come. The timing was exact and all happened in accordance with the Divine Plan.

On another, more personal level, you each had to deal with a deeper level of understanding that love does not die. It changes form and space, but it is everlasting. You are never abandoned by love. You are never really abandoned by your own heart. As you hold love for yourself within your heart, reflections of that love will appear to you from outside of you in many forms throughout your life on Earth. You all must understand this to grow, and you all have it within you to teach others about this kind of bond; to lead others onto a pathway of complete assurance that love does not fade. It does not disappear. It is not embodied in only one being. It flows from your own center outward and back to you again in one continuous movement. Picture the infinity sign. This is the symbol of love everlasting, and in the center of it is your own heart. Love is multidimensional, and it spirals into infinite space.

All of the women you mentioned above are souls you have traveled with for many eons and many lives here on this planet and beyond. They are not the only such souls, and as you begin to let your heart stay open, as you harness your eagerness and excitement, you will begin to attract the others. The bond between the five of you will not be broken; it will just expand to include many other kindred hearts. Feel this and embrace the feeling. Do not focus on the separation. It is illusion and somewhere in your heart, you know this.

Will you help me make the information we all received clear and relevant for others?

In time all of the information you received, and more, will become clear to you. For now, you are heeding our call and we are here for you. Keep your hand moving across the page and your heart and mind open. You will have all of the knowledge you desire. It is memory and connection; that is all. You were born with this knowledge, and we are simply sitting with you to remind you.

Rose: I was not allowed to speak my truth during my lifetime — too many rules and restrictions set up by my family, my religion, and the culture of my time. So in these pages I am speaking to you because you are an open channel. Not only did I want an education, I wanted the most advanced education I could get. I wanted to be a scientist or a mathematician. I was smart and I was silenced. From this place of understanding, my soul is at peace.

I am telling you this because I want you to appreciate the chances you have to speak up and to follow a path of your own choosing. It is important not to waste these chances. I know that you are now moving in Divine timing, or very close to this. I am here eager to join you in the world of human flesh. I feel that my choices were the best I could have made at the time. I am at peace with the lifetime in which you knew me. We prayed you down to make other choices and to open doorways for others that we did not have.

I am grateful for this chance to speak with you now. So many ideas and creations I could have offered were bottled up inside of me. I was obedient, I taught my daughters obedience, and I am telling you now to disobey anything that is an insult to your soul. Act up. Speak up. Make a ruckus. Have fun doing all of this. In Divine disobedience new things come in. By that, I do not mean you should disobey the Divine voice inside of you, but practice disobedience and disorder as your Divine right. I know you understand this, but sometimes you doubt yourself or hold yourself in line. This does not serve you. There is an inner compass built into you (and everyone) that tells you what feels good and what does not feel good. You know this — listen to it. Speak up without fear and stride boldly into the next phase of your life.

Hazel is silent for now. She is working in another realm perhaps. I can feel her love as I sit here. There is also perfection in silence. Perhaps that is her message for me today.

TIMING AND RESONANCE

1/7

The words "timing" and "resonance" are swirling in my head as I sit and listen for my grandmothers today. I had scheduled a marketing coaching session for my business at the beginning of this year, but weather and other unforeseen circumstances (on the coach's part) seem to be blocking my way. I have the feeling that it is a bit of Universal timing that is speaking to me. I am asking the Grandmothers today to tell me about timing and in particular, this bit of rearranging.

Hazel: The most important thing for you to focus on in this moment is this book. The writing of it, and more importantly, getting it out into the world. You have noticed a pattern of many things falling away in the last month. This is as it should be. They are not necessarily falling away, just stepping aside so that you may move ahead. This book is your main focus for now because it is a dream and joy of yours that can no longer be stopped. It is this way for many people when they come up against something that can no longer be denied. Things fall away to make room for the things of the heart.

When you are finished — and this means you must go through the harder work of putting this out there and asking for the help in doing it — other plans and dreams will come to the forefront again. The business coach can be a part of that. She is mostly the means by which you announced to the Universe that you are ready to step up. Once this plan was made, many wheels began to turn. The magic is in your statement, "I am no longer willing to be small." We applaud you. You are not small, nor are any of you currently residing within a body on the Earth. When you all begin to play large, everything will change.

The ancestors have paved the way for you. We were to be working from the other side at this time, but we see you and we are here to assist you from this vantage point.

Your business is who you are. As you get larger, it will grow beyond what you can comprehend at this time. Yes, the marketing coach can help to focus you; however, there is an energy at work that is beyond marketing. You have a teacher, Robert Young who speaks of an elevated platform of living. You are rising to this platform and much of what happens from this point is simply about resonance and flow. This is not a new story; it is being shown to you in a new way. Pay attention to timing — Divine or Universal timing. It is an important touchstone for you going forward.

I will speak to you now of movement. I can see the stagnation in your body. You must move to move forward. In addition to this time of writing, you must begin to move your body more. It is essential for you if you want to keep this body for a longer time. There are thousands of excuses to not move, but do it anyway. You cannot see how much this has to do with moving forward. Your heart will not fail you if you begin to give it more oxygen and some time to fully beat. Do not be afraid of movement. You need this body to fulfill your desire for being in it. Follow your inclination to move. Make opportunities to move.

As a side note, I am seeing my Grandma Hazel today as a pink mist. She is all love, and as someone who isn't particularly visual, I am finding it endearing that she is pink. It makes me smile.

Rose wishes to speak. I am seeing her as more red and purple. This is more of a feeling than an actual visual image. As I open to listen to Rose, she fades out and another voice comes forward. This new voice overwhelms me with feelings of love that wash over me in waves — like an ocean not a river. The feelings are on a higher octave than I have felt so far.

I am Mary the Magdalene. I have come through your grandmother Rose. She is stepping aside today so that I may speak. I am here to talk to you about love and about your own heart. For too long it has been closed in fear and resistance. You have met the love of your life and you are keeping yourself separate from him because you are afraid you will be lost in him. You do not want to bow to his will. I am telling you that when you bow, he will also bow. Bow to each other and thank each other for the finding and opening of love. It is a gift from heaven to find such love and you will blossom in the presence of it.

It is not possible to lose yourself in another. That is just your ego speaking. In death you will merge into One, when as a finished soul, you return to light. When you have the partner experience, and truly live it in the duality of "good and bad," you come closer to the finish, to the soul's great merging into One. Look at this person as a teacher, and ask him to do the same for you. It is in the asking and the breaking down of barriers that you will grow beyond what you can imagine. We have mentioned a lot about things that are beyond what you can imagine today. This is because so much is changing. As a visionary, you have inklings of this. As a human, much must remain in obscurity for the moment. It is not finished. It is never really finished.

Connect with this partner you have found on as many levels as you can. Help each other and evolve together. You have made much progress together in the past, and each of you can grow much easier together than apart. Pay attention to this. Open your heart to him. He has agreed to assist you in this life. No one can play large without assistance. Let him help you to fulfill his own agreement to have the experience of stepping out of the spotlight to allow another to shine. This kind of unselfish love is a gift freely given. Accept it and the Universe will open. Accept it and your heart will blossom like a rose.

I come to you through Rose. Your Grandmother was appropriately named. She could not fulfill her potential as you knew her and perceived her. She is not who you think she is. She will tell her story to you herself — she serves me and I her.

I can feel the Magdalene leave. Her energy came as a tone with words I do not understand. She is so loving but not in any way sentimental. Her love is sharp like a crystal, and laser-focused. I am in awe of her presence. Thank you to both of my grandmothers. You are a blessing to my soul.

BUSINESS PLANS: MOVING THROUGH RESISTANCE

Since I will be working on a vision for my business today, is there any assistance you can give me for this?

I am having trouble hearing, feeling, and writing down the wisdom coming through today.

(G): We are speaking. You are just resisting us. Take a breath. Open your heart and receive. Your vision is wide and deep, and it is not what the consensual reality necessarily accepts. Speak it anyway. You are a revolutionary. Embrace this role. Those beings coming onto the Earth right now will understand and embrace this. They are here for the very same reason. We spoke earlier of the children. This is one way in which you can support them. You have been here throughout this change. They need to know they are not here in a vacuum. There are those who have gone before who planted the seeds, just as we went before you to open up your space here on Earth. This is what the women do. They call forth the next generations who will affect the planet. Open doorways. Act in Divine timing and Divine accord to further life here and beyond. We are the bearers of the new. You have chosen not to have children because you carry messages and you had a different role in this life. This does not mean you do not plant seeds. You have simply chosen a different way to do this.

Keep in mind the importance of the children. Your message will spur them on and build them up. You are a messenger.

What about my business? I feel somewhat trivial bringing my grandmothers back to this question, but I realize and accept my humanness today.

Your business moves you around to spread the message. Crystals are a way of communicating beyond words. When words are no longer necessary, the crystals will speak on many levels. They are part of your gift. Go more deeply into this aspect and you will find many portals, many ways of communicating. You put more of your essence out into the world with the crystals. You have the energy and essence of the Elohim behind you. This is how you work. It comes through your smile, as you know. It comes through the healing and teaching work that you do. It comes through the crystals you send out into the world. Your business is a part of who you are. If you choose to be bigger, it will become bigger. Find the ways to put yourself in front of the people you want to teach. They will come if you make the first move.

We can feel your resistance once again. You do not really want to hide, yes? It can be frightening to put yourself forward, but it is frightening for many. Do it anyway and become an inspiration for those who also hold this resistance and fear. Have compassion for those who come to you. They too have broken through their resistance and fear in this act of coming. You are all in this together. Masters leading and teaching Masters. You are simply here to help others remember what we are helping you to remember.

You are all One. You have all walked this road before and will again. The children — many of them are new to this planet. However, they are ancient Beings. Understand that you can teach them to adapt. Or just remind them that there are those who see them and know their full brilliance.

Understand who you are, but do not put yourself "above." "I am another You." Know this. Know the reflection of your own essence in those around you. Breathe and relax in the beauty of this.

Rose: I will speak to you of organization. When I was alive, I kept everything in good order. There is an energy to this that I was not fully aware of. It allows the flow of ideas and a kind of peace that is not available in chaos. If you can organize your space, you can organize your thoughts. Ideas that were previously caught up in the chaos, open up and are able to move. Do not underestimate the usefulness of order in your life.

Order is not the opposite of freedom; it creates the freedom to move.

You often fear becoming like your mother in this way. Do not fear this. She has her own things to work through regarding order. She has created a mess that she cannot clear up. It gives her something to focus on instead of her pain. Let her be. You cannot fix her mess. You do not need to create your own.

There is a surprising amount of joy to be found in tossing out the old to make room for the new. Remember this. I wish I could have taught you more when I was alive. This was not to be. I was stuck in my own belief that I was "not up to par" because I had not gone to college. I will not belabor that point. What I could do when I was alive was to be orderly and create a beautiful space inside and out. That is what I did. I have no regrets.

Hazel: I loved to type. When I was typing, I felt like I was accomplishing something. The stories I told you kids when you were little were my stories. I never wrote them down but when I was typing I felt like a writer. It is a small thing, something I wanted you to know. My son John (who was killed in WWII) wanted to be a journalist and I loved to read his writing. He inherited my love for stories that I, in turn, got from my father. It gives me pleasure to watch over you as you write these words. My stories will come through you, not as I had planned them perhaps, but in a new way that is both you and me. My wish is that they will touch others. You have felt my hands touch in love and now others may feel the same through my words.

I am feeling a giant wave of love at this moment. I can almost feel my grandmother's touch.

Hazel: These words are for you and for many. Do not abandon this project. It is important for your growth. We cannot tell you how much we see you light up as your hand moves across the page. Keep going and see it through to the end. We will take it from there, and all of the power of heaven and Earth will be behind you.

DEATH

1/10

I am here in Wausau, WI (at my partner Robert's house), and I am trying to hear you. I am working in an unfamiliar place, so I am receiving static. I know it is my own resistance. I can feel my grandmothers' love surrounding me, but no words come forth. I am being guided to pick up the small amethyst skull on my altar.

(G): We wish to speak to you today of death. It is not exactly what you think and not exactly otherwise to what you think. It is a portal and a passageway. We are aware that you have been thinking that no one will remember you when you are gone. This thought is a concern of the ego and not the soul. It is similar to a body stepping down in vibration from a star or a galactic being. When you take on a body for the first time, you leave behind, temporarily, the soul group (and farther back, the star family) that you incarnated from. This soul group is a part of the One Creator, and eventually, all go back to the One. Your worry that no one will remember you is true and not true. Memories are stored in the body one takes on in any particular lifetime. They are a part of your [and any individual's] genetic line. On a deeper level, they are a part of your [and any individual's] soul group. The fact that there is no physical heir to carry forward your personal bloodline is not relevant. What is relevant, in the web that is life on Earth, is the soul lineage. More and more people are beginning to recognize this. You have what you call "family of choice" vs. "family of origin." This distinction is the beginning of the understanding of soul lineage in your current cultural age. As the word "family" begins to shift and broaden even more, your understanding of soul groups will further grow. As for remembering — no one needs to remember anyone else. All are sovereign and all are one when the last light blinks out on the Earth experiment.

Those who are drawn to you in love are your family, whether they pass through your life in a moment or you spend a whole lifetime with them. In the end, as you walk through the portal and into the light, you will be welcomed back. All will be folded and put away from this lifetime, and you will move on to other experiences with greater wisdom for the time you spent on Earth. Each series of lifetimes has its own set of things to experience and "learn" from.

I am feeling really sleepy at this point, and I can barely write these words.

The sleepiness you feel is the resistance to the concept of passing on without leaving an essence behind. Those who do leave their essence behind have become ghosts. It takes them time to re-collect and receive all of this essence back. You want to leave the Earth as you come in: pure, unattached, and unencumbered. All of the concerns of the ego can be set aside when you return to Spirit. When you are here with us, you are free. You are pure love.

We will tell you more about how to die as you come closer to death, and only if you wish it. It is something you have done many times as an Earthly soul, and it is not difficult. The difficulty lies in the resistance. So much struggle is attached to resistance. As you gaze at the skull, do not think of it as a part of you that is left behind. It is not this; simply think of your body as a hat left behind at a restaurant. Or something that fell out of your pocket along the way. The profundity of the skull is that it draws us into the concept of death, so that we become familiar with it. Become comfortable with the thought of dropping the body, like a suit of clothes and moving on. Feel the ease of this.

Cessation of breath is as easy as breath itself.

Hazel: Of all the losses I experienced in my life, the loss of my son was the most heartbreaking. It is something your mother has also experienced, and your father chose to leave his body early so that he would not have to experience the loss of his son. The part we do not understand when we are human is that love never stops. The part you are concerned with — who will carry love for me in their heart after I am gone — is an extension of that misunderstanding. The fear, "No one will grieve." There truly is nothing to grieve. When you are in a body, it is hard to grasp this. All of the talk we have given you about love — how it begins within and is just reflected back — is the lesson here. You are the love; all else is reflection.

This is a teaching you can use when those you love pass through the portal of death. To know that love does not disappear. It just takes on another form, both in this immediate life and of course, when you are rejoined in death — a continuum of love forming and re-forming within this lifetime and beyond. We will speak more of death. It is a concept that elicits way too much fear in life.

Rose: I struggled to cling to life for years beyond the point I chose to die. I became confused by life because I stayed much longer than I had originally planned. It became difficult for me to find the doorway and I became trapped inside my own body. This is the level of forgetting that is possible. This is the level of illusion and delusion that is possible when you resist death. I forgot who I was for a time (a forgetting that is even deeper than the forgetting of the body) and it became a struggle to become free.

She is showing me the time in the jungle when the portal opened for me. I went toward the light and was told in no uncertain terms that I had more to accomplish here on Earth. It was a deep teaching that I was able to go to the light without thinking and without resistance. I attribute this ease to the deep and intense energy of nature in the jungle — everything always in a state of decay or regeneration. Death just seemed a natural part of this process.

Rose: You had the right idea there in the jungle that day. The portal opened and you relaxed into it. You were sent back because it was not yet time for you to go. There was too much you still wanted to do at that point. It was a good teaching for you, however, on how to die. Relax into the portal. When your time does come, remember that day and it will be easy for you.

Sound will help you to pass through this portal of death. Call on the harp and someone to tone, and it will ease you into the arms of the angels.

TRUST IN YOUR OWN ABILITY

1/12

A while ago, my friend Katherine asked me to come up to teach a class on working with crystals in Wausau. Yesterday, I gave this class, and I've been thinking about it since then.

My question today is, "What do I need to add to my classes to make them better/more my own?"

(G): You must trust in your own ability to channel through the crystals and come up with ways of changing and enhancing energy for both healing and elevation. You must trust that you can keep an audience engaged for the entire time they are before you. Yesterday, we saw you shine. You were comfortable in your own skin and knowledgeable about the subject. You began your path of playing larger. It was a success and the Universe supported you in what you were doing. This is how it works when you make the decision to step up. You were able to plant seeds, and in some cases, light fires in people's hearts. This is no small thing. Feel this and spread the word. You will get the audience you deserve for the work going forward. A door has been opened — now all you must do is walk through.

How do I make this (referring to this book) about others and not myself?

Everyone has something they wish to do — that secret wish of the heart — that they may have been afraid of in the past, or that they do not trust themselves to do. Sometimes they just need an example, or the inspiration of someone else doing it, to take the first step. You can never know how a word of encouragement or a story told can affect someone. By sitting here and writing of your own struggles, and also your bright winnings over fear, you can inspire others to take their own dreams out into the open in trust and excitement. Remember your touchstone words for the year — eagerness and excitement. This was portrayed in your class yesterday and was felt by everyone present in the way they needed to feel it. You are rushing headlong into this new year. Keep the momentum going by remembering these words.

When things happen to deter your progress, they will not be enough to stop you if you can stay in touch with your inner eagerness and excitement.

I feel there is somewhere else you would like to take me today. Is this true?

Hazel wishes to speak. She is still a soft pink light in my vision. I can feel her love, but it takes a moment before I can hear her words.

Hazel: You can see the mastery in others but you have trouble seeing it within yourself. Why do you think Katherine (*who brought me to Wausau for the class*) wanted you to come and teach? She is a master healer. This is true. And, she recognizes the same in you. Do not be so quick to see in others what you cannot seem to grasp within yourself. Why do you think you have met two such women within the last year? (*Vicki Dodd being the other.*) It is because they are reflecting back to you your own mastery. You can also observe them and learn to navigate this knowledge with a great deal of grace.

These women are great teachers for you in humility and authenticity. They are huge essences, masterful healers, and down-to-earth women. Although they are those things, they are completely aware of their power. And, when they connect, they do so with intention and precision. Neither of these women need others to know how powerful they are, but they do not deny their power themselves. They own it. Look to either of them for inspiration as others will look to you for the same. Welcome to the world of reflection and mirroring. I am proud of you, as you are proud of many of your students.

When I was in the body of Hazel, I spoke in front of people in many different places. I always enjoyed every part of giving a speech or presentation — the preparation, the writing, and then the speaking itself. I was comfortable on a stage, and it was empowering to me to be able to travel and give speeches for the church. That was one of my gifts, and although it was in a small arena, it made me feel happy and fulfilled. As I watch you come into your own, I am delighted to see how your essence shines when I see you. I am cheering you on, and I am enjoying through you, the pleasure of teaching and inspiring.

Rose does not wish to speak today, but there seems to be someone who wants to speak through her. I can feel myself being pulled far out into a galaxy of stars. It is a different feeling than the Magdalene, and I am aware of the presence of tremendous light in the room. I am asking for words, as all I can hear at the moment are high-pitched tones.

We are your angelic guardians and we have chosen to speak through Rose today. We want to talk to you of the bridge you created yesterday (*in my class*). It is important to bring as many people as possible across that bridge in the next section of time. It allows people to feel, if only for a moment, the true nature of how things will shift. It allows them to get in touch with something larger than themselves, and to do that in a group where they are meditating or journeying for the whole. You cannot possibly grasp how much this will change lives. Do it and do it often. You might even do it in a more mundane setting such as a show. [*Note: The Angels are referring to one of the metaphysical shows I sell my crystals at.*] The experience will sink in as much as people are willing to let it, and it will leave no one untouched. If you ask us, we will assist you in making it possible in any venue you like. Explore this. There are many other things that can be done in this way. There is a brilliance to it that people can feel. It can bring in the vibration of joy to almost any group. So it did yesterday to the group that experienced it. You know the way over the bridge of heaven to Earth. You have traveled it many times. A door has been opened, and we are grateful to you. Gratitude moves and flows both ways, you know.

THE END OF STRUGGLE

1/14

Today I am filled with love and contentment. Everything seems to be flowing and I have no real questions for myself. Tell me about the end of struggle — about effortlessness and how it comes about.

(G): You are moving in different waters now and things will seem to move almost without thought or action. In the stream of love that is flowing through you today, you will find that everything is easier, brighter, and more fun. This is the place from which you can live your life right now. This place is not accepted by all humans, [as being possible or true] although it can be known by all. Not everyone has come here to experience ease. Not everyone is open to letting love flow through themselves. This is not a judgment. It is just what people choose to experience in any given lifetime. Some are here to experience struggle. All of you are here to experience the contrast between being in a physical body and being in Spirit form. This is the beauty of being physical — the contrast. You name it "good" and "bad" but it is neither good nor bad. It is simply what you have chosen at any given moment.

On a wider scale, it is the plan for your lifetime's experience. What you may not realize is that you can alter this plan at any time. When you have had enough of the struggle, you can choose to move beyond it. This involves giving up resistance to life and resistance to the feeling of love that you are experiencing today.

Struggle exists when you try to control your life from the outside. You have a tremendous amount of control about how you choose to look at something and almost no control over what happens outside of your own emotional/physical/mental realms. This is not a new concept, and yet many humans still try to control their environment. They will try to mold and shape each little thing that happens outside of them, and this creates great frustration and anger when things do not fall into place in exactly the way they had planned. You are familiar with this feeling because many times in your life when you are not "in the stream of love and consciousness" things do not work out as you had planned. The frustration you have felt at these times is your own attempt at control gone awry.

You understand this pain and struggle because of your own need to control things. You also understand how much easier it becomes when you simply let go and allow things to happen — no judgment, no resistance, no problems.

It is a choice people must make for themselves. You can lead by example, and you can create a field of love around you so that when someone comes into this field their struggle may ease a bit as they feel the energy of flow. This is really the only way to assist. Create experiences that bring joy and allow others into them. Then let go of the idea that you can change someone who does not want to change him or herself. In this way, new cycles begin to be perpetuated. It is not in your control, however. Just do what you do from love, and be content within that.

Rose: Think back to the times I tried to teach you how to sew. I was bound and determined to make you into a seamstress. It is a useful skill to have, sewing. I tried and tried to get you to sew a straight seam or to cut carefully from a pattern. You were impatient and wanted everything to be fast. Taking care and being precise were not your talents. It is not in your nature to take things slowly, or to be methodical. You were not a seamstress, and no matter how I tried (and I did try), you were not going to sew a straight line.

I see you now. I see your nature, and I know that all of my own frustration with you and how I thought you should be came from my own desire to control things. I know who you are, and from this vantage point, I see your strength. Hopefully, I did not make you feel too incompetent in trying to teach you to sew. It was done from love, and I know you understood that, even as a young girl. You just weren't about to turn yourself into something that you are not. It is the same with helping people to give up struggle. If they have chosen it for themselves, they must decide to let it go.

Hazel: I wish to speak a little bit about effortlessness — the other side of struggle. Effortlessness comes from being completely in the Now, outside of time and care. When you are completely engrossed in something, it becomes effortless. When you allow yourself to become fully engaged in your life, it takes on a degree of effortlessness that might surprise you.

Think of these words you are writing. You are just allowing the pen to move, and you have opened yourself up to the process. You are fully engaged with us and we are speaking through your pen. This is effortless. If you sat down and thought really hard about what to say, what others might think of what you say, or how to structure what you are saying, you would be staring at a blank page. Instead you sit down, call us to you, and just let your pen move. No thought, but completely engaged in the process. You have learned the secret to balancing being-doing. The secret to "Do nothing, but don't be lazy." In becoming engrossed and excited about the process, you have given yourself the gift of effortlessness.

DIVINE FEMININE

1/15

On this beautiful full moon in Cancer, I am at peace. I am still glowing from a beautiful circle where we blessed our work of the past year and the year to come. I am excited and eager to continue this journey. During the meditation in the women's circle, I was transported to Agra, the city in Northern India where the Taj Mahal is located. This beautiful tribute of a man's love for his dead wife contains a large monument fronted by water. I was taken to this pool in my shamanic journey, and we were to experience grace and blessing. Tell me about the still water at Agra, where my journey took me today.

(G): Today you opened a portal into the new Divine Feminine that is flooding your Earth at this time. The more open and receptive you all can become to this energy, the more balanced and whole your world will appear. Your group is one of many who are focused on this effort at this time. All of this energy is essential, and all of it is welcomed by Spirit. It is a part of the bridge — another aspect of what you create through your ceremonies and actions. You all are creating a new dance, and we see it as sparkles emanating from Earth. It is pure white sparkling energy, and it permeates all levels of your world and beyond. It is no small thing to come together in this way to create and initiate the miracle.

When we speak of the miracle, we are speaking of a new field of potential where creation becomes instantaneous. It will appear to you to be miraculous although it has been in your potential always. We are telling you to expect miracles on a daily basis, and they will be forthcoming. That is the energy you tapped into today as you sat and allowed grace into your body — as all of you did in your own way.

Groups of women have always created the changes and shifts that have occurred on your planet. The masculine energy has other tasks. They appropriated the credit for change from an ego standpoint. They appropriated many things, which threw everything out of balance. The feminine aspect was complicit in this. The feminine aspect within all people, both men and women, allowed this to happen. At no time was the feminine aspect's power taken away. Rather, it was given away. In this new incoming energy, balance will be restored. You chose the octahedron today specifically for this purpose. An octahedron is the sacred geometry shape of perfect balance. Calling it forth in meditation can bring this balance within. The balance you were feeling and the rippling out of that was not by accident. Balance will be restored, and it begins within each individual.

I am feeling confused at this point in the process so I ask, "What is this book about?" (I can almost hear them laughing.)

It is about women speaking up. It is about the time of manifestation in which you live. It is about an unbroken line (golden thread) of love passed from mother to daughter to granddaughter over eons of time. This love comes in many disguises and many forms.

The golden thread weaves it all together. We are telling you stories from our vantage point as Spirit, and also from our lives as human women. It is about how nothing is ever as it seems, nor is it otherwise. Think about that statement. It sums up duality in one line. We are telling you things that we were not able to say to you when we were in human form — things that we ourselves forgot when we came to the Earth. It is our sincere wish for you to open your awareness to these things not only through your mind, but through your deepest heart.

You will find the thread of the story as you re-read these pages. It will sing out to you. It will come together effortlessly, and you will have it out sooner than you can imagine. We can feel your skepticism. Do not resist this. You are opening to your full potential at this time. Don't close up now when you are so close.

Think of the threads you have questioned us about: love and relationships, timing, your business — not only career, but the business of living, struggle and resistance — the lineage and why we prayed you down. These are the big questions of life. We have told you about our lives in the hope that you would be able to learn and to see patterns that may not have been obvious to you as you lived them. Keep this story going as there is much we still have to say. We honor you for giving us a voice and we love you beyond time and space.

Hazel: Stories. Touch. Food. Sweetness. Your memories of me are touching. I was so grateful and amazed when you kids were born. You all took away some of my sadness about losing my son John in WWII. He would have loved you so, and he did love you from heaven. I was more [as a person] than your memories, and now I am everything in Spirit. The small wooden squirrel you have on your dresser is a touchstone for me. It brings me back into my physical life for moments. I can feel your presence and I am alive in your memory. It is a moment of sweetness. You say you do not remember the stories I told you about the squirrels, but they live inside that object. If you wanted, you could retrieve them. They are part of the fun I had when I was with you children — telling stories and watching your faces as you listened intently. These were acts of love. They are the reason we come into bodies, and they are the reason anything gets created (anything that is lasting and true). Remember my stories. Watch the squirrels. They remember the stories through their play.

Rose does not wish to speak today. I am so grateful to both of you whether in one voice or two. You are feeding me back my life, bit by bit, breath by breath.

THE THREAD OF THE STORY: WEAVING LOVE

1/16

Two days away from leaving, and my mind is on Tucson, where I will be working at the Gem Show for the next month. I'm going into the sun and warmth of the desert. After the cold and snowy winter we have had so far, it can't come soon enough. Also, I get to spend a month with Robert. I am really looking forward to that too. I was called to pick up the golden thread today. Why is this?

(G): You asked us yesterday about the thread of this story. We wanted to elaborate on this. Everyone wants to know, at some point in their incarnation, "Why am I here? What is my lineage and my connection to everything else?" We hear you question the word "everyone" in your mind. We will tell you that this is not the primary question of many. However, it is a question that comes up at one time or another for most. The people who will benefit from this book are bringing this question to mind as a primary question. We will tell you that by telling your own story (which is also our story), and asking your own questions, many will find a connection to their own story through you. Your friend Holly brought this up the other day when she reminded you that "your healing is my healing." This applies to all medicine stories and all medicine work. The golden thread runs through All That Is and connects all things together. It weaves in and out of time and eternity with precision and grace. You are tapped into this thread right now, and in so doing, what you write will touch all who have the awareness of this thread.

How is it so easy to become distracted from this task? Task, is of course the wrong word. It is more a pleasure to sit in this company.

(G): You have an active imagination and it takes you in many directions at once sometimes. The gift of clarity and focus comes with practice and discipline. This is not restrictive when you are truly focused on a project that brings you joy. Any body of work requires focus. This does not detract from freedom. You have made freedom a lifetime goal, and this is fine and beautiful. However, you have made the definition of freedom too restrictive. Ironic, no? Redefine your concept of freedom to include the freedom to employ discipline to a project that is close to your heart, and you will be amazed at what will happen.

You are and have always been free. This is your birthright, as it is the same for all who come into a body. Through your choices, your resistance to life, and your agreements on what you wanted to experience in this body, you have created the illusion of "no freedom" and limitations. It is time to redefine all of those things from a place of new understanding and more importantly, new feeling. You have always been free. Be free to be in a task that engages your heart, with focus and discipline. We will assist you as much as we can. The choice is yours to do the work (play) of this writing.

It is okay to be dreamy and distracted too. A lot can be accomplished by just letting your thoughts flow. There are no wrong choices — annoying, we know.

We do have more to say on the subject of freedom. Be careful not to define freedom as being free from relationships. You do not have to become entangled in another's karma (or drama) to be in a relationship. There are many relationship possibilities where both parties come freely and openly. You are in such a relationship right now, and you are still afraid that if you let yourself completely participate, you will somehow lose your hard-won freedom. This is not the case. Allow yourself to be wholehearted in your relationships, not just with your partner, but with everyone.

Your heart is whole and cannot be broken. This is the other side of freedom. To keep yourself out of relationship in the name of freedom can actually just be a cover for the fear of loss. This is not freedom. It is diminishment. We will ask you not to confuse the two. You are free to choose — love or fear. It always comes down to that.

I can hear my grandma Rose speak and then laugh. It is a high, clear laugh, like a bell.

Rose: Jeanie, my dear, you have denied yourself so much love out of the fear of a broken heart. You have created many situations to "prove" to yourself that love will break your heart. For the last fifteen years of your life, you have been working to clear your heart of all of this shadow and fear. At this point now, any breaking you feel in your heart is just phantom pain. Look within and see what is there. This is the jewel in the lotus. Your heart is clear and pure.

Love yourself from this clear place. We have said this many times; it is up to you to carry out this task. The fear is only a shadow. There is nothing substantial within the shadow. You are so ready to love with wild abandon — everything and everyone you meet. Do this and all of the magic of the heavens will be yours.

Hazel: You can feel the possibility of this kind of love as we speak to you. When you sit in your space with pen in hand, all is possible. It is just one tiny step from the pen on the page to the broader brush of your life. Go outside and meet your love. Find it in every face you encounter. We cannot say this enough — there is no limitation with love like this. Remember the Grandmother love you received as a child. This was our instruction to you on the purity of love. You were able to experience this because you have passed through many lifetimes of pain and sacrifice, and those lifetimes are over. Do not discount the work you have done on your heart. It has prepared you to leap, and the next step will be shown to you. Just as you allow this pen to move without thought or preconceived knowledge, so your life will unfold just by leaping into love. We are here for you always.

LISTENING

1/21

I have no particular question today, just the desire to reconnect and continue the thread of this book — whatever it is.

(G): Listen. You asked us in your prayer today to teach you to listen. We would like to speak about listening deeply. There is no greater gift that you can give to another person than to listen to them deeply without trying to form an answer, or correct what they say as they are talking.

To just sit and listen without an agenda, without judgment, is a gift beyond measure.

Witness what the person is saying, watch their eyes and feel their energy. Reflect back to them their beauty. Wait for your turn to speak, and then pause and drop into your heart before you give an answer or response. Ask people questions from the place that they are speaking and really listen to the answers. In this way you can get to know another deeply and meaningfully. This is the way of the heart.

Begin to know and appreciate the many different and unique ways that people have of expressing themselves. The many ways that beauty can be offered up in this world. Through this knowledge and this appreciation, balance can be brought into any situation. Within the talking circles you have participated in, there is the beginning of this deep listening and witnessing of others' wisdom. It is an essential part of any group dynamic that there be a time to listen and appreciate each individual in the group. The rule to simply listen without judgment allows everyone to feel heard. No fixing is necessary for all is perfection. In this way too, is the beginning of understanding. It is the best way to learn of your shared humanity and to know that you are not alone with your thoughts.

In any interaction where both (or all) people listen deeply, there will be a time when hearts will open, all parties will feel completely safe, and true healing, learning, and understanding will occur. This is a blessing, and this is one manifestation of true grace.

I am feeling the grace of this and my greatest wish is to be able to listen from that heart space and respond from there always. Why is this so hard?

When you were taught to listen as a child (we are speaking generally here, and not just to you specifically) much of what was being said to you was admonishment or the laying down of rules you were to follow. Many, many times the words "listen to me" were spoken in anger or frustration. This has been a pattern through the ages from parent to child. Many times it is for the child's protection. The intention is to teach or to keep them safe. The tone, however, is harsh or stern. Children listen to tone before intention, so the word "listen" becomes something related to harshness or even anger. You tune it out or turn away from it as a learned response.

This response is widespread. Listen — the word can imply that some restriction is about to follow. Your response is rebellion or resistance because you want to remain free of restrictions. This is just a cycle that has been perpetuated and can be broken through awareness. When the words "listen to me" are spoken from a true desire to be heard and understood, they will come to mean something quite different. One of the ways this can happen is to begin to use the talking circle with very young children. They are open and loving, and they will accept that way of teaching and responding readily. Teach by example. Listen to the children with complete acceptance and non-judgment, and they will learn to listen in this way too. Important seeds can be planted with the children. We have said this before, and we will repeat ourselves often in this respect. Listen deeply and with love to the children coming forward, and the world can change on a dime.

Rose wishes to speak — she is very starry today. I close my eyes and I can see the galaxy unfold before me.

Rose: My Jeannie, you are unfolding like the spiral of stars you see before you. In this practice of sitting with us each day, you are coming into a potential that was not laid out for you within this life. You have completed much karma here, and you have lightened yourself to an extent that anything can come next. I want to give you words of encouragement here, so that when, or if, this process becomes difficult in the next stages, you will keep going. You have learned to open your heart and listen to us without any preconceived plan. We are grateful to you for listening.

I was not often heard in my family simply because I was a woman. I associated the word listen with being undermined. It was my duty to be quiet and accepting of whatever was said by my father or my brothers. Listening was not something that was ever reciprocated to me. When I did speak, I was not listened to with respect. I was not heard in my life, and I am grateful to be heard as Spirit. Even from this place of understanding, I can access the feeling of not being heard. It is one of the hardest things for one to face. Listening with respect and complete attention is an act of love — radical and deep love. Remember this.

RELATIONSHIP AND CHOICE

1/22

Deep breaths today. I'm feeling a need to relax a bit. Being in Tucson with my partner (we do not live together the rest of the year) is challenging. I am trying to get used to the energy of another around me all the time. I am trying to do this with grace and not necessarily succeeding.

What can I do? How do you incorporate relationship into a solitary life?

(G): You have had the luxury to choose how you live your life. It has not always been easy living with your choices. You have chosen at this time to explore a relationship because it is one of the primary means of growth on the human plane. This is where you can look into the mirror of the Other and take the measure of your reflection. Your primary relationships reflect back to you how far you have come and the necessary distance you need to travel to meet your own goals of growth. Those things you see that are the most problematic to you are those things that you must either accept or change within yourself — not in your partner.

This is the same situation as having clients come to you who are working on the same issues you are. There is no accident in this. It is simply the Universe reflecting back to you what you most need to see in a particular moment. Do not become attached to these moments. Become aware. Acknowledge them and take them in as instruction and not judgment. Do not judge yourself in these instructive moments. Interpretation or some awareness of your own issues will ease the way in a relationship. You are examining these things through us at this time. Bring your awareness both inward and outward at the same time. This is the way to growth.

Through the relationship you have at this time come the questions that you need to ask us. And through the questions come the necessary awareness for growth. It is a progression. He sees you whether you want to accept this or not. He sees you and he loves you for all that he sees. Accept this and return the loving acceptance to him. Let yourself go and you will find many things to learn about yourself in the process. We are laughing now because you resist this so fiercely. You are not giving up a piece of yourself; you are gaining so much awareness through the reflection of The Other. Remember, the more he annoys you, the more you are seeing your own reflection. Opportunity is everywhere.

I can hear Robert talking loudly on the phone in the other room. This is really annoying me. I can feel myself resisting my grandmothers' words.

(G): We are sensing your annoyance at this intrusion. We will point out that life is intrusive. The better you are able to handle the messiness and chaos of life and still keep your center quiet (and carry on with what you need to do), the more you will be able to accomplish. In your heart you know that this may just be an excuse to avoid doing the work you are being called to do. Do not use the interruptions and intrusions to your peace to avoid doing this work. Having another around will be a challenge. Accept the challenge and keep moving.

We have used the word acceptance a lot in our conversation today. Pay attention to this. In this word — acceptance — is the key to relationship peace. Acceptance is a two-way street. It does not mean that you must change anything; simply accept the fact that the Other is there for your own growth and edification. You have not put yourself in a situation where there will be anything unacceptable. Remember this and pay attention to where you are not accepting him for who he is. Others may put themselves in situations, such as abuse, where the lesson is to stand up and to not accept. This is not your situation. You are working with a clear mirror, and your lesson in this situation is to accept the other wholeheartedly and to ask the same for yourself.

I ask my grandmothers if there is more to this because I think it is making me uncomfortable. I have always had a problem with the Universe being a complete and unadulterated mirror reflecting back my inner thoughts and feelings. Though I know this is true in my mind, I resist accepting the truth of it, especially when things are not going my way. There it is. Control. I can feel my grandmothers laughing here. All of this has been said from such a loving place that I can feel my body relaxing into the awareness without too much resistance at all.

When you relax into the acceptance of your life just as it is, you open up a space for change and growth.

This is how change happens. Softening into acceptance takes away all of the resistance and all of the desire for control. This is how real change always happens — by relaxing into the space you occupy, looking around for what engages your heart, and moving in that direction. Easy.

NEED FOR ENCOURAGEMENT

1/23

Today I am beyond tired. I didn't sleep last night, and I am trying to get used to a life with Robert where all is "do, do, do" with little time to just be. I know this is part of my work now, and I must find a way to incorporate him into my life. I am not sure what the question is today. Maybe I am running out of questions.

(G): Go back to the beginning and find the thread. We have prayed you down so that you may experience the full range of experience that is life. We are not here to tell you how to live it, but we would like to remind you to enjoy it for the big mess of feeling and experience that it is. Don't get ahead of yourself. Just be with what is in front of you at this moment. If you are feeling tired and low energy, then slow down. Don't force yourself to do anything. Even this time with us, don't let it become just another chore. We are encouraging you to get this done because we know the joy that it will bring you and the sense of accomplishment. On days when this is just another chore, put it aside. We will be here when you return refreshed and renewed.

I feel self-indulgent and whiny with these questions sometimes. Tell me about your lives and when you most needed encouragement.

Rose is making herself known. I am getting the impression that she was a wild child stuck inside of a devout upbringing, which allowed her little freedom. I remember a time when I accompanied her to Pittsburgh to see her daughter, my Aunt Norma. She was driving down the turnpike, and at the time the speed limit was fifty-five. We were talking and she was driving. A cop pulled her over for going eighty-five. She actually talked her way out of the ticket. I can't remember how she did it but as we continued on our way, she looked at me, smiled, and said, "I like to go fast." On that day, I began to look at her a little differently.

Rose: You have found me out. I loved the freedom of driving the car, and going fast always seemed risky and dangerous. I was allowed so little freedom in my life, and most of the time, I was quiet and did what I was told. What I really wanted to do was go to college, become a professional (I liked numbers and science) and make my own way in the world. I didn't marry your grandfather until I was quite old [twenty-eight], at least in the time I lived. I liked being able to take care of myself. I put myself through secretarial business school and became a bookkeeper. It was not really what I had in mind, but I did it myself and I was proud of it.

I did not receive much encouragement. I was supposed to marry, have children, and become a good wife. I loved your grandfather, and I resented the life I led at the same time. For years I made myself content with it. I let anger and resentment overtake my life in my later years. This was my decision, not consciously made, but made nevertheless. I can tell you now that life became very small, the more I let the anger eat me up. It took my mind in the end. All that was left was the anger. I am telling you this so you can learn from my experience. You can let anger overtake you, even when you are not aware of the cause. It is okay to feel anger, just let it out in a constructive way and then don't hang on to it.

I am at peace now, and when I come back, I have chosen to experience the letting go of anger. Life will create experiences for me to learn about letting go. While you are alive, you can choose in any moment to let go of anger and resentment. It is a peaceful and much more joyful choice.

Hazel: I did not receive encouragement from anyone when I was growing up. My mother was just trying to keep food on the table, and my brother always had one foot out the door. My father was long gone at this time. What I did to help me feel less alone was attend church. In that time of worship, I felt close to something larger than myself. I could connect with a loving Father and feel that love while I was there. It was a comfort and an encouragement to me to feel this presence that was greater than myself. You feel it in a different way, but it is the same energy that you are feeling.

My church, and the work I did for it throughout my life, was my encouragement, my solace and my strength. You find this in nature, and that is another way to do it. I always knew when I was alive that you would find a way to connect to God that was very different from mine. I also knew that once you did, it would bring you as much comfort and encouragement as my church did for me. Your father could not see this, but I knew.

Be at peace with the choices you have made. Let yourself expand into them and really feel the love that is present within the energy you have connected to. I can see your sparkle as you connect. It does my spirit good to see this in you.

PURPOSE

1/24

It feels like I am running out of questions, or maybe I am just "off" today. I am trying to adjust to the rhythms of a new place and to living in close quarters with another person. The question I feel under all of the uneasiness is about the word purpose. When I am out of my element, such as when I am here in Tucson, my certainty fades and that word haunts me.

(G): You have gone back to the original questions, and this is a big question of many people, especially those who are on the spiritual path. "What is the point and purpose of this life I have chosen? And, how can I make it more meaningful?" Just by asking the question you (and anyone who asks it) have opened yourself up to a more meaningful existence. When the question is posed to the Universal Light, your personal matrix lights up in a way that is like a beacon to individuals and experiences and will lead the way to meaning in the manner to which your soul will respond.

I can see this light in my mind's eye, but I have no words to match what I see.

We are trying to simplify here. This process involves light, sound, and an energy signature that draws the next set of circumstances for your soul's enjoyment. By asking the question, the answer is set in motion. Many of you do not trust the process and feel that you must find something "out there" to teach you or to tell you the deeper meaning and purpose of life. This is all fine, and it is one way to begin the process of going within. However, going within is the key. What will give a life meaning and purpose is always found within that individuated soul. You can begin the process by looking outside, but it will always eventually lead you back into the limitless inner dimensions of your own soul.

For my own edification, are the tools of sound and light (crystals and sound instruments) helpful to this process? Is this my purpose for working with them?

(G): We will say that these tools have only just begun to open to the wider human world. You have come here to spread them around or offer them up to those who are ready and willing to employ them for expansion. Keep playing with them to do your own inner work and to create ways for others to be introduced to them. You cannot tell another Being what their purpose is in this life — no one can. You can make it easier for them to access their own inner dimensions, as long as they are willing to walk down the road that opens up before them. Create experiences and don't be attached to how they are experienced by others. Every soul who incarnates here on Earth knows the purpose of their existence. It may be forgotten or unclear while in the body, but the driving force of the soul will always guide them to where they need to be.

So, in answer to your question — yes and no. Up and down. Use them or don't use them. Your own soul knows. Does this road you walk bring you more eagerness and excitement than it brings pain? That is your question. As you explore the deeper meaning and purpose of life, this must be your (and everyone's) question. Pleasure or pain? Love or fear? Go toward love and you will automatically find meaning and purpose open up for you. It sounds simple, and it is as simple as you choose to make it. If the experience of "difficult" is one you want to explore, that might be a way to explore meaning and purpose. It is not mandatory.

Hazel: Do not discount the way you were brought up. Look for the meaning underneath the meaning. Find the kernel of truth that lies within all pathways to God. Follow that, and take it into your heart. The human experience is deep and wide, and all things are valid within it. Your roots are deep in the tradition of Love, whether it is the Christ or the Magdalene. Tradition or Transcendence. Look to both and you will transcend all. We will speak more of this — the kernel of truth is that all pathways lead to the same place. You know this but do not yet understand it. Open up to All and you will know.

TRADITION AND TRANSCENDENCE

1/26

I want to ask more about what we started to talk about at the end of yesterday, but I am not sure where to begin. Tell me about tradition and transcendence.

Hazel: When I was alive, I was deeply connected to the Christian tradition. My work was my church and beyond, but always in the confines of the Christian religion. I led the women's society and went so far as to lead it on the state level. I volunteered with the YWCA. I understood, in some way, that this was what was available to me at the time, and I loved what I did. I also knew that as women, we sustained the church. Without us, it would not have had nearly the outreach and appeal that it did. I did not aspire to be a minister or hold any of the male roles. It did not even occur to me to do so. In many ways, I was a very traditional woman although I rose quite naturally to leadership roles within the confines of what I did. I felt proud of what I accomplished, and I was happy when I was traveling around for the church.

Serving the Lord. It is a phrase you recoil from, but I did not. It was something I did joyfully and it made me feel whole. Serving something outside of myself and my family was a privilege that I was happy to accept. As I see things now, I understand that God/Source/The One Love is within each person who incarnates into a body. I also understand that through my service as the woman Hazel, I was incorporating that Source and embodying that Spirit of One. There was no differentiation — no wrong or right involved. I was simply following a road that opened to me, which brought me closer to God/Goddess.

What you do not understand when you recoil from your traditional upbringing is that it also brought you closer to that One, which is beyond human understanding. It was your first way into the understanding you now possess about Universal Love, Energy, and Flow. Honor where you have been, no matter what, because it has brought you to where you are now. There is no wrong way to come to this understanding or relationship with Source energy. I am using different names here to illustrate how many ways there are to come Home.

Tradition can be (and in your case, was) the entry point into transcendence. Consider those who must find their way to Spirit having no connection to it in their early years. They have a much harder time finding the pathway or even having an awareness that a pathway exists. This was the original purpose of all religion — finding and connecting to that which transcends where you are, the smallness and limitation of being human. Traditional religion is merely a starting point and one that I am grateful to have been a part of.

You see my life as having been limited; I see it as having fulfilled my purpose for coming. Do not shed tears for me as a woman unfulfilled. In many ways, your broader range of choices has left you more directionless. None of this is good or bad. It is just the way things have progressed. I am telling you to honor and bless the tradition you came from, and move in your own way into transcendence. This is the time.

Rose: I am leading you once again into the angelic realm from whom you are descended. You will hear only tones for a moment as we adjust our vibration. Listen to the birds outside of your window and you can attune to us as well.

As I listen to the birds, their songs and the tones I hear become words. I can feel a similar energy to what I felt when Rose spoke from the angelic realm.

In this place, you will no longer need to understand. It is beyond understanding. We are just allowing you to feel it open up inside of your body. There is nothing left here of what the mind can grasp. There is music and tone. There is light fractured into many colors. This is Home. You may come here through sound and crystal. This is why you must continue to disperse your crystals. They will lead many beings closer to their own ideal Home, both here on Earth and beyond. We will lead you to the necessary crystals. You have only to ask us and we will assist you in choosing or finding the stones that sing. You have done this in the past, and we are grateful. However, the crystalline realm has amplified many times over in the last few years and there are stones that are ready to work with humanity at this time. This is a part of what you can do with your gifts — attune others into the dance, the flow, the "elevated platform" of life on Earth.

Open up and let us guide you to where you need to be. We are here to serve the Elohim of which you are a part. You do not need to say this. We can feel your resistance. You only need to Be it. As Hazel has said, it is neither good nor bad. It transcends all of that. Keep your eyes and your heart open to how the stones speak. When they sing to you, pick them up.

I can feel the completion of this time with my grandmothers and the angels. From here, I have no idea where we will go. I don't think this is a book about stones, but they inform much of what I do. So they are never far from the radar.

PHYSICALITY AND RESISTANCE

1/27

I feel physically drained today, and I am not focused on a question. What is happening with my body, and how can I make it relevant to these offerings?

(G): The fact that you are in a physical body is both a blessing and a curse. You can feel the limits in the body that your spirit knows are not really there. It is part of the dichotomy. Learning to thrive and grow within those limits is the task of each human being, no matter where they are in the continuum. Time, although it is purely a construct of man, has grown out of the limits of the physical plane. It was put in place organically as a measure of the days and hours of light and dark.

I am not receiving this channel very easily. I have put a restrictive limit on myself today, and it is interfering with the flow of this information. My head is heavy, and my hand can't move. What is happening here?

(G): It is resistance. It is the stopping of flow — just as you were becoming attuned to it, just as you were relaxing into it. It is your ego mind bringing you back to [the state of] stuck and stasis. This is the point where you can break through. This is the point of choice. We are here with you and will continue to be. Are you willing to step up, or are you not? There is no shame in either position. It is your choice to continue. Your body is just supporting the resistance at the moment. It may be wise to take a few days and just do nothing, without guilt or shame. We are always with you and you are very close to a completion of sorts. We have told you enough to put in a book. You can begin the work of revision and organization. More will come as you go into this process. We are overseeing from above and if you wish it, we will organize with you. It will not be as hard as you think. Let your physical body rest when it needs to rest. Do not be so frantically pushing. All will be completed in the Eternal Now.

TRUSTING THE FLOW

1/28

I am here in Tucson at the Gem Show, and the chaos of my life at the moment is not allowing me enough time. I am unable to give this writing project, that is dear to my heart, the time and attention it deserves.

Why do these projects and inspirations always come up when I am away and unable to deal with them?

(G): Why do you think this chaos will stop when you "returning to your life"? Why are you not trusting of the flow of goodness and prosperity into your life? Do not be in fear about this. Do not buy into the belief that things will stop when you return. They are just beginning to open up and there is great possibility ahead. Embrace what is coming (the new year in general). Do your best to respond promptly and reconnect when you can. Trust your life.

You made the statement at the beginning of the year that you no longer wished to play small. The Universal Source is responding to this declaration. Let it flow to you. You have worked your whole life to come to this point. Open to it. We are repeating these simple words so you will realize how simple it really is.

Just open to your own gifts and miracles will happen. Time is elastic; play with this elasticity. See how far you can slow down one second or speed up an hour. We are playing here. Be light. Life is not a serious task; it is a joyful experience, no matter what happens within the short moments you are on the Earth. Enjoy yourself, no matter what you are doing. Your beloved said it well when he gave the mantra "I am happy." For as you say it and believe it (choose to believe it), so shall you be. It is the same for prosperity. Feel it. Breathe.

Rose is showing me a pattern and a motion sequence that I don't know how to put into words.

Rose: I am showering you with rose-gold light. This is an influx for which you are ready. It will lighten your spirit and increase the amount of light you are able to hold. You are currently among many sources of amplification [the crystals in Tucson]. They amplify the energy that surrounds them so there is much chaos and contradiction in the surrounding energy. This light will help you to discern and hold high light forms. Diamond light if you will. It will keep you balanced within the chaos. There are tools you will find here [at the gem show], and pieces that must be passed along through your hands. The rose-gold infusion you are receiving will help you to find your way within the chaos. Accept this gift from me and from the Elohim family of which you are a part. We are with you, and through you we flood the Earth with the rose-gold light of the highest Love. Be at peace and move through these days with ease and grace. This is the fulfillment. We will speak more of this. Just know that you hold keys, both within your abilities and within the crystal tools you use. All Beings hold their own keys. Hold them with grace.

I am so grateful for all that has come my way, for my beautiful grandmothers, Hazel and Rose, and the lineage from which we all come. Thank you.

MOVEMENT AND TRUST

1/30

Today I am in the Flow — no recriminations, no questions. I am Here Now.

What would my grandmothers like to say to me today to begin to weave these threads together into gold?

(G): Just begin. Take action to move yourself from one place to another. This is a moving time. The time that has gone before was a time to just Be — to go within and clear the muddy water of your soul. Now it is time to move with clarity and precision, making each step a purposeful one. Even if the only purpose is to move your physical body, movement is key right now.

The other component of this movement is complete trust in yourself, in the Universe and in us if you wish. It is an old saying to take the leap and the wings will appear. Is this not so? Well, it is a truth that you can absolutely trust. You have made many strides in developing trust in what you cannot see. Keep going in this direction and you will find the miracles you desire.

There is still some hesitance on your part to completely trust your voice. We are speaking through you and this book will be shaped by your voice and your ability to trust yourself. There are other places where you must open up and use your voice. We would say to you that this [using your voice] will move you farther than you can imagine in this pivotal time of movement. Do not be afraid to speak up. Let others hear the wisdom that is Jean. We prayed you down, but you have called us here so that you may speak. Sacred reciprocity — always at work, and always balancing everything that is. It works in all things. Remember this.

The time for practice is finished. You know all that you need to know to move forward. The angels are at your back, by your side, and everywhere you turn. Lean on us when you need to. However, you have your own wings now. Use them.

Resistance can and has become a habit for you. It keeps you in your comfort zone. You cannot have movement and resistance at the same time. It is not possible. Right here by simply keeping your hand moving, more will come to you. Do not stop to think. Just move your hand. We will guide you.

What are some concrete ways to overcome resistance? Are there other ways besides movement?

(G): Breath is another way to move. Even in complete stillness, the breath moves in and out. Focus on this when no other movement is possible. It will do a lot to move you through resistance. As will the decision to simply let go. Accept where you are in this moment and let go of your resistance to that. Do not desire to be anywhere else.

Dancing is another way to move through resistance. Sound is the perfect way. You have not used the sound exercises recently.

My grandmothers are referring here to the exercises learned through the Sacred Sound School run by my teacher Vicki Dodd, who has profoundly affected me in many ways.

The sound healing techniques take care of both moving resistance and using your voice. Two birds. You have the tools to move yourself elegantly through the rest of your life. Use the many things that are available to you. You have not learned these tools just to assist others. You have learned them first and foremost to assist yourself.

When you return home and are not restrained by time, use the sound each day and see what happens to both your movement and your voice.

Rose: I have said this before, and I must say it again. When you do not use your voice, when you hold your tongue for much of your life, you become angry and bitter. Most of that anger is at yourself for not having the courage to speak your truth. It can be directed outward to everyone you meet. It can also eat away at you. Do not let this happen.

I was paralyzed by my own fear to speak up and by the learned behavior of my childhood that told me I had nothing worthwhile to say (as a woman). I had to allow myself to become demented in my last years in order to release the anger I held. This was hard on my family but necessary for me so that I would not carry the anger into another place and time. When I passed from this life, I was complete with the anger and will not have to experience it in the same way again. It was my soul's choice and it is done. I am telling you this so that you may speak. Much of what you have done with anger shamanically has released your need to follow my path. Still, you must speak because you wish to be heard in this life. You have much to say and it can touch many others. Let yourself speak.

COMPARISONS

1/31

Today is the second new moon of this January. I am so tired, I can barely think, much less channel through words of wisdom. I am here nevertheless because I have promised myself that I would keep at this until I am finished. I am here because this is important to me. I am willing to receive whatever wisdom I can today. I am grateful for it all.

(G): We feel your exhaustion, and we will be brief. Do not worry so much about the day-to-day aspects of this book. It will come to completion as you make yourself available to this place of openness. Although the commitment is important, do not beat yourself up if you miss some days.

Do not compare yourself to others who are on the same path you are. They will find and pursue what they need and you will do the same for yourself. Do not let anyone make you feel "less than." This is something we see you struggle with much of the time. Your gifts are unique and extraordinary (as are the gifts of all the other Beings on the Earth). Let them unfold and flower without the hindrance of comparison with others.

One of the saddest things we see is the constant comparison of one Being to another and the feeling of "less than." This is not the truth for any of you.

We are seeing you wander from this space. Your brain is filled with worry and feelings of overwhelm. Remember, there is time for everything. Remember that Now is all you have or will have. What do you want to do right Now? If it is to worry about all that you have to do, this is fine. If it is to continue to work, this is fine too. We are here. You are here for all eternity. Step back and consider this. There is all the "time" you need contained within eternity. It is a large feeling, little grasped by those in human form. Do not worry so much. Things will be done in their own time. Remember to enjoy the experience. Let yourself be in light. We will stop for today. This is not something that adds to your worry. We are here. We are in Love.

Hazel: I see you. I see your heart and it is opening in its own time. Let yourself breathe for a moment. If I was in physical form, I would scratch your back right now and just let you relax under my hands. Even though you were a "touch me not" as a child, you have become one who loves to be touched. Imagine how far that has taken you. Look at how you have opened. Feel my hands at your back — blessing you and touching you with the biggest Love you can feel. As your Grandma, this is how I loved all of you kids — purely and completely. This is how I love you still from this place of no-time.

I am feeling this perfect love, and all I can do is breathe.

NAVIGATING ANGER

2/2

I am angry with Robert this morning. I don't have time to ask a question. The grandmothers just begin.

(G): You must navigate your life in rough water as well as in calm. Do not judge your response to life. Just notice and be aware of where you find yourself. There will be times when you act from anger and frustration, and this is a part of the experience. Allow it to move through. Express it if necessary and then move on.

Step back from your anger for a moment. Thousands have gone before you in this feeling. Thousands will experience it in the future. It is a small moment within a small moment that you experience now. Step back and let yourself feel the infinite within this moment. Breathe in the steam from your tea and close your eyes. Swim with us in the eternal waters and wash yourself clean of all that has gone before and all that you are feeling right now. There is only this eternal Now.

Expand. Lose the edges for just one moment, and feel and remember what you want to do with this time [my hour for writing]. Expand outward and take in the experience of no edges — nothing sharp to hook into, nothing old to grab ahold of. Just float with us for this time. Let go of the mind completely. It will be there when you return. Soar. Spin. Drift in this state of edgelessness. You will return to this space soon enough, and all of the small moments will fade into rosy glow. Life is full of simple experiences felt to the fullest and then gone. The specific experience does not matter. From where we are, you can see far into the fabric of light that is woven from the original thread of one's existence. All things appear as small sparkles within this matrix of light.

My Grandmothers *are showing me the beauty of this vision of the journey.*

When you feel these moments of frustration and anger, step back and remember what we have just shown you.

I have just spoken of how tired I am and how I am sorry to have given so little time to this project since I have arrived in Tucson. I can feel the love they have for me, and I know without a doubt that they will be waiting patiently for me to sit down once again to finish this. I am so close and I can feel them cheering me to the finish line. My gratitude knows no end in this process.

GOING BACK TO THE THREAD

2/3

I am in a stuck place today. I know it is my own resistance.

Teach me to listen — to move my pen without thought or preconception.

(G): Too many questions today. Remain open. We have said we will be with you through the entire process. Now is the time to rest. Take a break and return to this with new eyes and "beginner's mind". You have come halfway through and there will be more. The process will weave back and forth until you are finished. Remember the gold thread you were given at the beginning. Now is when you take the thread and weave it through all of the stories and offerings on these pages. It will be as simple as creating a braid of hair. Do not resist the process of synthesis; it is what you can do here. It is what you have always done. Bring together strands of light. Anchor them into the place where you are — Earth, in this incarnation. You have been many places and in many forms. This story is of the Earth.

Grandmother energy is of the Earth. We are solidly rooted in our lives when we are here on Earth. When you become an elder, you have had time to anchor — time to have had the experiences that teach wisdom when one is open. At the very least, you are able to relax into your life just as it is — to accept where and who you are. If you are not able to do this, there will be disease, dementia, and even death.

Grandmothers who grow into and cherish their roles are loving and wise. We know this does not apply to everyone; however, the energy of "Grandmother" the archetype, is one of loving care. We are of the Earth. We use what is on Her with care. We nurture and sustain Her. We keep Her alive through our gardens, our bread and our stories. Even those who do not have children can access Grandmother energy through an open, giving, and loving heart. We embody the Divine Feminine as crone, as wise woman. Our job is to care and to spread wisdom born of a thousand different threads of light, woven together as our lives.

Grandmother remembers history. She tends her garden because she loves the feel of the dirt in her hands. She makes bread for the same reason. These are gifts of gratitude for a life well lived. When we do not have this, we offer other gifts of our own experience, no matter the manner in which they are given.

We are the lineage of love, spread through the fabric of life on the planet. We are wisdom. We are the dark fertile ground. We are the flowing waters. We are the gardens of great beauty. All of these things and more are embodied in the energy of Grandmother.

Jeanie, as you come into your own wisdom years, embrace the gifts you have been given. You make words sing. You carry the wisdom traditions of your current lineage and those lineages you have chosen down through the ages. You tend the Earth through your love and understanding of the stones. Embrace these gifts and pass them along with love. Trust yourself. You are Grandmother.

Hazel: When I had to write a speech, I would just sit down at my typewriter and begin. It either came or it didn't as I sat there, but the act of sitting down was enough to begin the process. Even if I got nothing out of that sitting, it began the process for me. The speech would be written, usually the same day. As I watch you sit each day, pen in hand, I am so proud of you. I can remember the anticipation I felt, just sitting down at the typewriter. My son John wanted to be a writer, and I like to think he got that from me. My words were limited by my experiences. Your words (or my words through you) are now limitless. I love you beyond all words, and you are writing now for many who have not been able to sit down and do it. Whether through circumstances or resistance, there are many who never can sit down and get it done. Write for these people. Inspire them. Give them a voice. John died before he was able to fulfill his promise. Write for him. He is here as well, within the One Light. We are cheering you on. Just sit down each day and your promise will be fulfilled for all of us. As with releasing pain for [all within] your ancestral lineage, so it also is with attaining fulfillment for your lineage — two sides of the same coin.

TUNING IN

2/5

I have *no questions today. What is it that you would like to say?*

(G): Be open to what you are doing today, whatever it may be. Transfer your aliveness (or infuse your aliveness) into each thing you do and each encounter you have. Allow yourself to just enjoy whatever situation you find yourself in. This aliveness will energize you and those around you.

You are tuning into people's exhaustion. Tune in instead to where they might hold enthusiasm. Be intentional with this. Find this space and pay attention to it. You will be surprised at how much better you will feel. Do not try to change those around you. Just recognize that there is a wide space within each of them to feel joy, vitality and enthusiasm. Meet them there.

I am having difficulty recognizing and feeling their joy. Is it not that I am taking something from them?

(G): You are just looking and listening deeply. You are seeing a part of the essence that you all share. There is nothing to take and nothing to give; it is a bottomless well. By seeing it in others, you can activate it within yourself. This is hard for people to grasp because each body seems so distinct. The oneness can only be felt for moments at a time. It is the truth underlying your existence. When you can grasp this concept of Oneness more and more, you can tune into this joyful and energetic place often.

This is how empathic ones or psychics, who are in their integrity, seem to know or see your situation and life. They just align with the Oneness and speak from that place. In reality, all of you can do this. Align with the Oneness that you are, and then speak from that place. Within that place, there is only Love. We speak to you in the same way. We differentiate from the Oneness for a moment to speak as someone familiar to you. It is the love you recognize out of all the Love there is.

My mind is wandering now. I cannot hold this Love and this concept for very long. My ego breaks in to remind me of "Jean."

When I let myself feel this much love, I get sleepy and want to break off. Why?

(G): You must remember that you deserve this much love. You came from it, and you will return to it when your body passes away. The sleepiness is just resistance in another guise. You turn away from love because you feel you do not deserve it or that somehow it will be taken away. This is not the truth of love. It can never be taken away. Love is within you and all around you. It will always come back to this. We will remind you of this no matter how many times it takes because it is the truth of who you are and where you come from. No one can take this away. There is an infinite amount of Love and this is true for All. It cannot be said enough and there will never be too many ways to say it — not until each soul knows the truth of it. It can expand, but it will not contract. The laws of physics do not apply to love, not as you understand them.

COMING TO THE END

(G): We have spoken to you through our words and our stories of our perspective from on high.

> **Through the stories of others, we all come to see how our own story weaves into the One — each story unique, each resonant with the other like a musical chord with many tones blending into one.**

Through these words we have transmitted our love for both you and for all. As we draw to an end here, know that nothing ever ends. There is an ocean of love, endless and flowing. At any point, which is always Now, you may call us. We have said we will assist as you weave and re-weave these threads to make one whole.

When you get stuck, please use your voice in any way you can. Use the tones, the hum, and the sounds of your own body as it connects with the ground to come to clarity and pick up the thread once again. These tones connect you to your lineage, which goes beyond what you can imagine at this time. Use them. Use the stones you work with to do this as well. There are many tools available to you.

Do I have so many blue stones at this time to remind me to use my voice?

(G): The blue stones will help you connect with the voice that has been trying to sing since you first drew breath. You are drawn to blue at this time because you are finally beginning to speak. Let yourself be heard. Do not be afraid. We have spoken to you about fear and resistance (which is an aspect of fear). Use these words to inspire others. It is a simple thing.

One other thing we must say about this process of writing. Do Not Compare Yourself To Others. It is soul-killing and silencing to go to the place of comparison. Every voice is unique and there are many stories to tell. Your voice and stories will resonate with others just as other people's words resonate in your heart. Heart to heart you speak, and with open hearts, others will listen. This is how the Universe works and this is how resonance works.

When you go to the place of comparison, stop. Take a walk and listen to the birds. Take some breaths and do the dishes. Do something else that requires movement and not thought. Let your mind rest. Come back to the task when your mind is turned off and your body has been in motion. We cannot overstate the importance of motion. Let your pen move across the page just as it is doing now. Let each word be a surprise and leave your mind open to whatever comes. Trust yourself to speak.

I am wondering about and fearing the experience of loss when I speak my own truth.

Rose: I am another you. Are you prepared to see this? Have we said enough that you begin to see how this works? You had the thought about loss just now. Yes, I lost much in my life. Like you, I lost siblings. I experienced that pain and that sadness. I buried it deep within me because as I have said before, I could not speak. We did not speak up in my house. By speaking now and being heard, you have broken the spell of silence — the kind of silence that is enforced and buries thoughts and emotions deeply so that they can never be spoken. You have allowed both Hazel and me a voice, and although we no longer need it, we honor you for breaking the pattern of fear and repression in the familial lineage.

I am at peace now, all of my anger and frustration gone, spent in those last years of confusion and rage. I have chosen to remain in peace for a while. You felt you had seen me as my great-granddaughter. This is not the case although there is much of me in her. I watch over her, and she will go her way as she chooses.

I am stopping now because my mind has gotten in the way. I am grateful to you, Rose, for all you have taught me both in body and otherwise. I am grateful for your stories and I am grateful for your love. Rose has said she will speak more of loss on another day. Hazel will speak another day. I have apologized for being so scattered, and in response, the rosy pink glow of love that is Hazel has amplified so I am filled with love.

REPRISE

3/12

I have called you in once again after a month's hiatus. I have felt your presence, and I needed to settle my life back into the rhythm of Chicago in order to continue. The year started off really promising, and it still has much promise. But in the last few days, things have fallen apart. I can't get my classes to work. I know I need to really step out there and know my own worth. To not hesitate as I offer them, but it is so hard to release the thought "no one will show up." I have tried to let it go, and I am at my wit's end. Even as I write that, I know there is more that I can do. Help me to see the way forward. Help me to release this weight of "not enough." I am asking today for your help, knowing that the answers are within me. I will be most grateful for any guidance you can offer.

(G): When you remember your true lineage and take it into your heart, you will be free. It is so simple — you are a child of the Light. You are here to shine. We can help you see this, but you must take into your heart and Be it. You are not in a place of trust right now. You are becoming desperate to achieve something, to prove yourself or to compete with some idea of what a "spiritual person" is. What you have to offer cannot be compared to any other offering. It is unique, and without it the world will be poorer. Don't measure yourself against others. There are no scales, no yardsticks in heaven — all is Light. Each light shines equally with its own brilliance.

Take time each day to feel this. You can see and feel it in the moments when you connect. Get back to the Source of your own wisdom, which is the Source of all things. It is as you tell others. You must meditate, even if it is only a few minutes per day, to connect with the timelessness of Eternity, to connect with that place within you that is the Divine Spark — that makes you "you."

We have been with you always, but we have come forward at this time because you have been given a clear voice and a way to state things that can touch people. Do not discount your voice. You have told others of the blue stones you have gathered recently. This is no accident. Use the energy you have connected with so profoundly — that of the crystal beings — to help you now. They are about finding truth. Use them to bring forth your own truth.

Believe in your magic. Embrace it. This is not a time of burning, no matter what it may look like. There are signs of opposition to the magic that exists at this time. Ignore them. What is being put forth in the public media is not the Truth of what has occurred over the last decade or so. Look within to know the Truth. Look at what you have surrounded yourself with, and look into your own heart. There you will find the truth.

Where do I need to be?

(G): Everywhere. Use the technology of the time to expand. We are supporting expansion at this time. You have been given the tools of expansion. As with all tools, they can be used in duality. Look to the light at this time. Though duality is and has been necessary, there is no need for you to dwell there any longer.

Your physical presence will be moving as well. We will tell you to move toward Love. You must decide what that will look like. Your heart knows this. We are grateful for your assistance always. We cannot move in the Earth field without all of you who remember and hold this vibration. We are grateful and we are you.

We are standing on either side of you. We will help you to perform your next task. It is what you came here to do. Do not let fear stop you. Yes, you will always feel fear within this human body. The trick is to go ahead and act anyway. Do not let it paralyze you. Look at what you have done so far. You are speaking up in front of rooms full of people. And they are taking it in. Keep going. Keep planting the seeds. As a Grandmother, you are in charge of planting seeds. Your seeds are not of the plant kingdom. They are of the crystal realm. Plant them anyway and know that they will grow. We are here with all of the love you can take in.

AFTERWORD AND ACKNOWLEDGEMENTS

I began this book almost two years ago and I feel compelled to say that my life has moved forward in a beautifully synchronistic way since then. I did move from Chicago to Madison, WI to be with my partner Robert. The business is growing and thriving, and I can honestly say that life is good. I credit the loving guidance from my grandmothers for many of these positive changes.

I would like to thank all of my teachers and students who have taught me so much through the years. Thanks to Susan Lipshutz who gave me the original assignment to sit with my grandmothers and listen. Much gratitude to Oscar Miro-Quesada, Francisco Montes-Shuna, Isabel Chinguel and Olinda Pintado, Quinturrey, Vickie Dodd, and all of my non-human guides and angels.

Deep gratitude to Christine Thom, editor extraordinaire, for her valuable insights and understanding. Thanks to Jesse Krieger at Star of Light Publications for his clarity and focus in bringing this book into completion.

Thanks to my sistahs Barb Q., Piper, Holly, Kay, Maureen and Lois who are my heart and who keep me sane. Thanks to Cindy Starry for her lightning flashes of insight and her support.

And, the most loving thanks to my family and my partner Bob who taught me about love from day one.

GRANDMOTHER WISDOM:
GIVING VOICE TO YOUR OWN STORY

You know when you feel like you have so much wisdom inside of you, and you would love to give it voice or write it down, but you are afraid to speak up or to put your wisdom out there for the world? Feelings like:

- What if I have nothing worthwhile to say?
- What if I go my whole life with a story inside of me and it never gets told?
- What if I let me fear win out and never speak up?

At the end of this class, you will have your own story down on paper, video, or canvas.

Connect with your own "grandmother wisdom" in this 8-week class. Here I will help you to overcome your fear and resistance to speaking up, and to write, film or paint your way out of it. To connect with your own guidance and intuition in a way that speaks to others. To find your own voice through writing your way out of fear, writing your way out of pain, writing your story to heal yourself and others.

As my grandmothers pointed out throughout this journey, since we are all One, the experience of each individual — when told to others — can be a teaching and a healing for All.

For more information on this 8-week journey to writing, speaking or drawing your own wisdom,
go to www.wisdomofthegrandmothers.com.

FINDING YOUR PATH TO LIVING YOUR WISDOM
A 7-MONTH TRANSFORMATIONAL JOURNEY

This course goes deeper into some of the main topics of **Wisdom of the Grandmothers: Tips for Living from the Realms of Love.** It is about finding your authentic path and living from a place of deep wisdom. We will explore in depth:

- Using your intuition to connect with your own lineage for healing and growth
- Working your way through resistance
- Not. Being. Perfect.
- Loving yourself and creating your life from that place
- Creating abundance from a place of love
- Moving through transition and change with grace
- Creating your path to joy

At the end of this journey, you will have a clearer idea of where you came from and why, what your path on this Earth is, a map of how to work through resistance to joyfully move onto this path with ease and grace.

Each section of this transformative course will contain guided meditations, journal questions that we will discuss on live Q & A calls, exercises and positive action steps to work with, a private

Facebook group to create community through the process and beyond.

You will also have access to one group call per month in addition to the Q & A, and a ticket to a live event in the summer of 2017.

To receive information and sign up for this journey of transformation go to www.wisdomofthegrandmothers.com.